Acknowledgements

The idea for this book originated with Stanley Wells and Peter Holland, who invited me to contribute a volume about Shakespeare and the Bible to this series. The kind and meticulous comments of Peter Holland at every stage of composition provided confidence and guidance. Two National Endowment for the Humanities summer seminars produced unique opportunities to learn about the book's twin subjects—one on Shakespeare with Stephen Greenblatt at Berkeley and one on The Bible as Literature with Leslie Brisman at Yale. Robert Miola read early drafts of several chapters and offered useful advice. I am indebted to colleagues at Cal Poly University, San Luis Obispo, California, for granting me a term's paid leave in 1996 and to students in both my Shakespeare and my Bible as Literature classes whose responses helped me frame the book's design. Graduate students Elizabeth Brunner and Craig Whitt furnished excellent research assistance. Melody DeMeritt supplied indispensable help with copy editing. Hilary Walford and Sylvia Jaffrey corrected errors in the typescript with precision, perspicacity, and patience. Frances Whistler, editor at Oxford University Press, was extremely generous with her time and talents. As always, while working on this project I have gathered sustenance from the wit and wisdom of my wife, Jan Howell Marx. The book is dedicated to the memory of my father, Henry Marx, who lived from 19 April 1906 to 31 October 1995.

| Oxford Shakespeare Topics

Shakespeare and the Bible

Oxford Shakespeare Topics

GENERAL EDITORS: PETER HOLLAND AND STANLEY WELLS

Shakespeare and the Bible

STEVEN MARX

OXFORD

UNIVERSITY PRESS

OXFORD
UNIVERSITY PRESS

Great Clarendon Street, Oxford OX2 6DP

Oxford University Press is a department of the University of Oxford.
It furthers the University's objective of excellence in research, scholarship,
and education by publishing worldwide in

Oxford New York

Athens Auckland Bangkok Bogotá Buenos Aires Calcutta
Cape Town Chennai Dar es Salaam Delhi Florence Hong Kong Istanbul
Karachi Kuala Lumpur Madrid Melbourne Mexico City Mumbai
Nairobi Paris São Paulo Singapore Taipei Tokyo Toronto Warsaw
and associated companies in Berlin Ibadan

Oxford is a registered trade mark of Oxford University Press
in the UK and certain other countries

Published in the United States
by Oxford University Press Inc., New York

British Library Cataloguing in Publication Data

Data available

Library of Congress Cataloging-in-Publication Data

Marx, Steven, 1942–
    Shakespeare and the Bible / Steven Marx.
        (Oxford Shakespeare topics)
    Includes bibliographical references (p.   ) and index.
        1. Shakespeare, William, 1564–1616—Religion.   2. Religious drama,
English—History and criticism.   3. Religion and literature—
History—16th century.   4. Religion and literature—History—17th
century.   5. Bible—In literature.   I. Title.   II. Series.
PR3012.M37   2000
822.3′3—dc21   99–38704
ISBN 0–19–818440–9
ISBN 0–19–818439–5 (pbk.)

3 5 7 9 10 8 6 4 2

Typeset by Kolam Information Services Pvt Ltd, Pondicherry, India
Printed in Great Britain
on acid-free paper by Biddles Ltd, Guilford and King's Lynn

Contents

List of Illustrations

Fig. 2 by permission of the Shakespeare Centre, Stratford-upon-Avon; figs. 1, 3–4 private collection: with gratitude to Jonathan Byrd's Rare Books and Bibles, www.great-site.com

General Note

The translation of the Bible cited throughout this book is one that most authorities agree Shakespeare read, the Geneva Bible. Produced by a group of Protestant exiles in the Calvinist city of Geneva, this English translation is heavily framed with editorial apparatus, including letters of greeting to Queen Elizabeth and the reader, prefatory summaries of books and chapters, maps and illustrations, and a running commentary in the margins. It was published in many editions and is still preferred to the later King James translation by some Protestant denominations today. A facsimile of the 1560 edition was published by the University of Wisconsin Press (Madison, Wis., 1969).

Citations to Shakespeare are to *The Complete Works*, ed. Gary Taylor and Stanley Wells (Oxford: Clarendon Press, 1994).

Biblical dates are given as CE and BCE rather than AD and BC, in accordance with standard scholarly practice. 'Old Testament' and 'New Testament' are employed when these terms are used or implied by writers under discussion. In other cases, the terms 'Hebrew Bible' and 'Christian Bible' are adopted to conform with contemporary scholarly conventions.

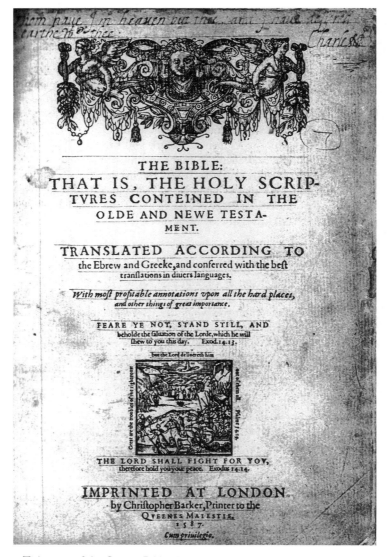

THE BIBLE:

THAT IS, THE HOLY SCRIP-
TVRES CONTEINED IN THE
OLDE AND NEWE TESTA-
MENT.

TRANSLATED ACCORDING TO
the Ebrew and Greeke, and conferred with the best
translations in diuers languages.

*With most profitable annotations vpon all the hard places,
and other things of great importance.*

FEARE YE NOT, STAND STILL, AND
beholde the saluation of the Lorde, which he will
shew to you this day.   Exod.14.13.

but the Lord deliuereth him

Great are the troubles of the righteous

see Iohn 28.   Psalm. 7619.

THE LORD SHALL FIGHT FOR YOV,
therefore hold you your peace.   Exodus 14.14.

IMPRINTED AT LONDON
by Christopher Barker, Printer to the
QVEENES MAIESTIE.
1587.

Cum priuilegio.

1. Title-page of the Geneva Bible, the annotated version that Shakespeare read.
The first edition was published in 1560; this edition is dated 1587

1

Introduction: 'Kiss the book'

'Kiss the book', slurs Stefano, the shipwrecked butler, in Act 2, Scene 2 of *The Tempest*. Spectators see him sharing a swig of wine from his homemade bark bottle with the drunken savage, Caliban. The words that he travesties with the language of the tavern originate in the house of worship, where they refer to a loving connection between a reader and a text. 'The book', in English, signifies only one book, the Bible.

Since 1623 that pride of place has often been shared with one other book, the *Comedies, Histories and Tragedies of Mr. William Shakespeare*. People travelling westward in America usually carried both. In the 1840 journal of his expedition from the outpost of Detroit into the wilderness of Lake Superior, one explorer wrote that, on a typical sabbath day of rest, 'We read the Bible I dare say much more than we would have done had we been in Detroit. Shakespeare was duly honoured, as he is every day when we travel. When on the water, some one of the party usually reads his plays to the others.'[1] For other readers, the order of precedence is reversed. In an 1895 memoir about her father Karl, Eleanor Marx wrote, 'As to Shakespeare, he was the Bible of our house.... By the time I was six I knew scene upon scene ... by heart.'[2] But, whatever the priority between them, in relation to all other books, Shakespeare and the Bible remain together unequalled.

The first edition of the King James translation of the Bible was published in London in 1611. It is unlikely that Shakespeare had a hand in this project, but not impossible.[3] The first collected edition of

Shakespeare's plays, the Folio, was published only twelve years later. Both are opulent volumes. The King James Bible originally sold for about £4 and the Folio for about £1, roughly equivalent to £800 and £200 ($1,600 and $400) in 1998. In the early 1990s, copies of the 1611 Bible and the 1623 Folio fetched £38,000 and £380,000 ($65,000 and $650,000) respectively.[4] The Bible's Epistle Dedicatory to James raises him to godly status: 'Your very name is precious among [your people]: their eye doth behold You with comfort, and they bless You in their hearts, as that sanctified Person who, under God, is the immediate Author of their true happiness.'[5] The dedicatory front matter in Shakespeare's Folio does no less:

> But stay I see thee in the Hemisphere
> Advanced and made a constellation there!
> Shine forth thou star of poets and with rage
> Or influence, chide or cheer the drooping stage;
> Which, since thy flight from hence, hath mourned like night
> And despairs day, but for thy volume's light.[6]

There are many more illuminating connections between what is inside these two volumes, but until now no critical book has been dedicated to their study.[7] This conspicuous absence may be partly explained by an inherited Romantic view of Shakespeare as a supremely secular poet, the embodiment of 'the human and dramatic Imagination', in contrast to Spenser and Milton, who exemplify the 'enthusiastic [i.e. visionary] and meditative Imagination'.[8] It may also have something to do with an aversion to 'Bible study' among academics, who associate it with sectarian preaching.

Wordsworth's distinction does not recognize that the Bible permeated Shakespeare's imagination as thoroughly as Spenser's or Milton's, though in different ways. This is demonstrated by Naseeb Shaheen's three-volume catalogue of biblical quotations, allusions, and echoes in the plays, as well as by the prominent biblical themes in *Measure for Measure* and *The Merchant of Venice*.[9] As to Bible study, since 1980 an exciting new field of literary criticism of the Scriptures has attracted secular scholars such as Robert Alter, Harold Bloom, Northrop Frye, and Frank Kermode.[10] These writers bring sophisticated techniques of reading literature to their study of the Bible, revealing some of its rich, subtle, and grand features. As Alter says, 'we are in fact better readers of biblical narrative because we are lucky enough to come after Flaubert and Joyce, Dante and Shakespeare'.[11]

While a literary perspective enhances reading of the Bible, knowledge of the Bible informs any reading of literature. Nevertheless, as Frye observed, 'many manifestations of the Western literary tradition, because they are formulated in terms of biblical imagery, biblical plots, specific verses from the Bible, have become unintelligible to contemporary readers'.[12] Most students know more about the *Odyssey* and the *Aeneid* than about the Old and New Testaments. My own education provides an example. As a teenager I pored over the first three chapters of the Bible in Hebrew School, but I was exposed to no more than Genesis and the gospel of Matthew during a rigorous undergraduate and graduate course of study based on the Great Books. It was only after earning a Ph.D. and teaching Renaissance literature for several years that I became aware of the gap in my own education and tried to fill it by preparing an English class on the Bible as Literature. After doing so, I could make more sense of Spenser, Milton, and Blake; and I began to understand parts of Shakespeare that had long left me puzzled. So I decided to experiment with a course on Shakespeare and the Bible. It turned out that in ten weeks it was possible for students to read five plays and six books of the Bible— enough to find their way around both large volumes and to discover how each illuminates the other. That experiment led me to write this book.

2

Any imagination being formed in sixteenth- and seventeenth-century England would have been saturated with what was the most powerful cultural influence of its time. T. W. Baldwin states that young William absorbed the Bible through a grammar-school curriculum that included much scriptural reading, including some in Latin and Greek.[13] Shaheen disputes this claim but observes that compulsory weekly attendance at church services during which lengthy passages were read aloud guaranteed that all citizens were thoroughly familiar with Scripture. Showing that most of the passages cited in the plays were not to those biblical books that were used in the liturgy or to the translation recited in church, but rather to the widely distributed

Geneva Bible first published in 1560, he concludes that Shakespeare spent a good deal of time reading the Bible in private.[14] The Reformation had encouraged individual reading of the Scriptures as essential to salvation, but, during the reign of the Catholic Queen Mary from 1553 to 1558, William Tyndale, the first Protestant translator of the Scriptures, was burned at the stake along with hundreds of copies of his recently printed work. Mary's Protestant successor, Queen Elizabeth, reintroduced Bible reading as both a religious and a political duty, 'kissing the book' herself in the course of a public ceremony at which she accepted a copy of the Bible from the allegorical figure of Truth and promised to read in it every day.[15]

Elizabeth's successor James sponsored the government project of a new translation not only to pursue his own devotional and scholarly interests, but also to support the heavy ideological structure of divine-right monarchy. He devoted considerable resources to expensive cultural productions of all sorts—triumphs, pageants, masques, holiday celebrations, executions, pardons, and religious rituals. He did so to display and memorialize himself, and to counteract resistance to policies he wished to promote—policies that drained money and power from other interest groups in the commonwealth. Along with other absolutist rulers and political theorists in early modern Europe, James cited the Bible to summon God's support for his claims of authority over the civil and personal lives of his subjects.

In the 'Argument' prefacing his own book, *Basilikon Doron*, James wrote: 'God gives not Kings the style of Gods in vain | For on his throne his Scepter do they sway.'[16] His favourite biblical model was King Solomon, who extended the Israelite empire created by his father David, brought peace and prosperity, was himself a scholar and poet, and sponsored a vast programme of support for the arts and sciences. 'God hath given us a Solomon, and God above all things gave Solomon Wisdom; Wisdom brought him Peace, Peace brought him riches, riches gave him Glory', wrote Bishop Montague in his introduction to James's collected works.[17] Francis Bacon dedicated *Novum Organum*, his programme for the reform of learning, to James as Solomon the Wise and called his Utopian University in New Atlantis 'Salomon's House'. Rubens depicted James as Solomon on the ceiling of his Banqueting House, a building designed by Inigo Jones as part of a grand scheme, never completed, to rival the same divine-right aspirations of those who commissioned the Sistine Chapel in Rome, the Escorial in Madrid, and the Louvre in Paris, all of which supposedly followed the architectural plans for Solomon's Temple set forth in detail in the Bible's Book of Kings.

An essential part of this campaign by the baroque court to glorify the absolute state and 'metaphysicalize the person of the ruler' was played by theatre.[18] James wrote that 'A king is as one set on a stage, whose smallest actions and gestures, all the people gazingly do behold.'[19] His performance of this dramatic role in public spectacles displaying the ruler's ability to cure diseases with the magic touch of his hands was reluctant, but he relished the chance to appear on stage in masques in which he was simultaneously divine actor and spectator.

The Banqueting House was home for many such dramatic productions. The most prominent feature of this theatre was what was called the State—'a raised platform with a canopy for the King and his most honoured guests . . . its position . . . made it possible for all the spectators to see the king while he talked or watched the play'.[20] It was also sited as the only perfect observation point for the play's many painted sets. Here the monarch occupied the same position as God in the Revelation of St John, sitting on the throne among his elders watching one pageant after another.

Another element of theatre that appealed to absolute rulers was dissimulation and disguise, the opposite of spectacular display. Claiming to imitate the biblical Christ who 'emptied out' or relinquished his essential divinity to appear among mortals, monarchs were to be regarded as divine beings costumed as human players moving among their subjects.[21] But the humiliation of experiencing fallible mortality also reinforced the royal sense of their actual superiority, and it justified lying, spying, and other forms of manipulative behaviour secretly carried out on behalf of the welfare of the nation. A contemporary, Sir Anthony Weldon, wrote that James's private motto was 'Qui nescit dissimulare, nescit regnare' (He who does not know how to dissimulate does not know how to reign).[22]

In addition to providing a source of political propaganda, during the Renaissance the Bible became an object of humanistic scholarship. Lorenzo Valla and Desiderius Erasmus unearthed, compared, edited, and published ancient biblical as well as classical manuscripts. Pico Della Mirandola and Marcello Ficino searched for a common source for the writings of Homer, Plato, and Moses that would provide a key to universal symbolism. Niccolò Machiavelli read the Bible as history, in the same way that he read Livy and Tacitus, looking for information about the development of the Israelite state, about military strategy, and especially about the way founders and leaders used religion as a means to achieve political goals.

The Renaissance Bible was also appreciated as a great work of literature and an artistic inspiration for writers and painters. King James's favourite preacher, John Donne, rhapsodized on the beauty of God's style as an author: 'thou art a figurative, a metaphorical God ... in whose words there is such a height of figures, such voyages, such peregrinations to fetch remote and precious metaphors ... such curtains of allegories, such high heavens of hyperboles, so harmonious elocutions ... as all profane authors seem of the seed of the serpent that creeps; thou art the dove that flies.'[23] His enthusiasm was shared by Sir Philip Sidney, whose impassioned 'Defence of Poetry' against puritan iconoclasts celebrates the literary accomplishments of 'David in his Psalms; Solomon in his Song of Songs, in his Ecclesiastes, and Proverbs, Moses and Deborah in their hymns; and the writer of Job'.[24] Michelangelo, Caravaggio, and Rubens pictured Old and New Testament subjects no differently from those in Greek mythology—with glorious, naked renderings of the human body, psychological realism, and dynamic energy informed by imaginative readings of their sources.

Such aesthetic appreciations of Scripture were as controversial during the Renaissance as when, in the book of Ezekiel, God threatened those who listened to his words only as poetry: 'And lo, thou art unto them, as a jesting song of one that hath a pleasant voice, and can sing well: for they hear thy words, but they do them not. When this cometh to pass (for lo it will come) then shall they know, that a Prophet hath been among them' (Ezek. 33: 32–3). The controversy still continues in debates over the acceptability of treating the Bible as an academic or artistic subject rather than Holy Writ.[25]

A related controversy concerning the question of how Shakespeare himself regarded the Scriptures, whether he was reverent or irreverent, whether biblical references in his plays support, challenge, or satirize Christian doctrine, has dominated much previous discussion of Shakespeare and the Bible. Answers must remain tentative, since, as Alvin Kernan observed, 'Shakespeare took his politics, like his religion and his philosophy, to his grave with him.'[26] Given the dangers involved in maintaining any religious position during a period of sudden and violent shifts in what was considered orthodox, such reticence was only prudent.

One school of interpretation reads Shakespeare's biblical references as a didactic reinforcement of Christian doctrine that utilizes the media of drama and poetry to support theological points. Arthur Kinney states that '*The Comedy of Errors* intends, with one [biblical] reference following another, to direct us away from the farce of a world of men who are foolish in their pursuit of fortune and family when they forget about God and towards a sense of comedy such as that conceived by Dante.'[27] He argues that Shakespeare's stagecraft was derived from the popular liturgical drama he was exposed to in childhood—a form of theatre supported by ecclesiastical authority to engage people with scriptural stories in order to increase their allegiance to the Church. G. Wilson Knight states that 'the unique act of the Christ sacrifice can . . . be seen as central' to the tragedies and that Shakespeare's 'final plays celebrate the victory and glory, the resurrection and renewal, that in the Christian story and in its reflection in the Christian ritual succeed the sacrifice'.[28]

Such orthodox approaches have been countered by strongly worded opposition. A. C. Bradley held that Christian theology is irrelevant to Shakespeare's writing and that any biblical references in the plays represent merely human behaviour and nothing about God or the supernatural.[29] Roland Mushat Frye wrote a book entitled *Shakespeare and Christian Doctrine* specifically to debunk the interpretations of those he dubbed 'the School of Knight', sarcastically punning on the name of a reputed conspiracy of Elizabethan atheists. He argued that 'Shakespeare's intent is essentially secular, in keeping with what sixteenth-century theologians would have expected from literature.'[30] Late twentieth-century critics surmise that Shakespeare, along with his contemporaries, was involved in an overall cultural movement that funnelled the energy of religious forms and expressions into various temporal replacements. Debra Shuger reports that 'in Foucault, Greenblatt and other contemporary thinkers one notes a growing interest in the passage of sacred forms and practices . . . into the social and literary structures of secular culture'. These 'mythic transformations' were possible, she observes, because, 'in Renaissance practice, the Bible narratives retained a certain . . . flexibility . . . a sort of extra-dogmatic surplus of undetermined meaning—or meaning capable of being determined in various ways'.[31]

Shakespeare's texts themselves offer evidence for both sides in this controversy, sometimes with different interpretations of the same passage. In *The Winter's Tale*, Paulina says to onstage and offstage audiences, 'It is required | you do awake your faith' (5.3.94–5), just before the statue comes to life in one of the scenes Knight sees as enacting Christian 'resurrection and renewal'. The action takes place in a chapel and the moment has the solemnity of high mass, but the miracle that ensues is shown to be a staged illusion. Falstaff, 'that old white-bearded Satan' (*1 Henry IV*, 2.4.463), is constantly quoting Scripture in order to justify his own engagingly amoral behaviour and to mock any form of self-righteousness. But his antics become steadily less charming and he dies crying, 'God, God, God,' and babbling what may be a reference to Psalm 23 (*Henry V*, 2.2.9–20). And Shakespeare's worst villains delight in feigning reverence for Scripture, all the while letting the reader in on their treachery:

> But then I sigh, and with a piece of scripture
> Tell them that God bids us do good for evil;
> And thus I clothe my naked villainy
> With odd old ends, stol'n forth of Holy Writ,
> And seem a saint when most I play the devil.
> (*Richard III*, 1.3.332–6)

3

The ambiguity of such allusions and the credibility of both orthodox and sceptical critics leads to the hypothesis that Shakespeare read the Bible with a very wide range of interpretative responses to its vast plenitude of meanings. A corollary premiss is that Shakespeare imitated scriptural models with the kind of variety found in later biblically inspired writers such as Milton, Dryden, Blake, Hopkins, Mann, Kafka, Faulkner, Kazantsakis, and Beckett.

No playwright could encounter, say, the stories of Ruth's midnight courtship of Boaz (Ruth 3) or Jesus' sojourn with the disciples in Emmaus (Luke 24: 13–53) without appreciating their dense dramatic textures. Such highly wrought passages are not rare in the Old and

New Testaments. As Alter says, 'There is evidence of ["the high fun of the act of literary communication"] in almost every line of biblical narrative ... the lively inventiveness ... repeatedly exceeds the needs of the message, though it often also deepens and complicates the message.' When that inventiveness and complexity are not obvious, 'Language ... is fashioned to intimate perspectives the writer would rather not spell out and invites our complicitous delight in the ingenuity of the fashioning.' Demanding and rewarding such imaginative complicity from actor or reader are hallmarks of Shakespeare's style. In addition to a general spirit of literary free play, Shakespeare found subtle techniques of storytelling: varied transitions and contrasts between incidents, recurring motifs and correspondences between parallel incidents, and a carefully controlled variation between disclosing or obscuring characters' thoughts and motives, to name just a few.[32]

Like Sidney, Shakespeare recognized the range of literary genres by which biblical books could be classified and the elaborate rules of composition and comprehension such genres imply: in Genesis, a combination of creation myth and prose fiction; in Exodus and the succeeding books of Numbers, Deuteronomy, Joshua, Judges, Samuel, and Kings, a cycle of national histories; in Job, a tragedy; in Ruth and Esther and the gospel narratives, tragicomic romance; and in Revelation, a masque.

What might be expected to exclude books of the Bible from being considered in the same category as other literary works is the Scripture's emphasis on God as its main character and author. Extrabiblical representations of God were forbidden by Jewish tradition and opposed by Wycliffite preachers. However, medieval miracle plays brought God on stage in three of his biblical roles: creator, saviour, and judge. The actors playing those roles trod a thin line between dramatic credibility and sacrilege, while the scripts referred to the 'character' both as 'Saviour' and as 'Figura' or metaphor, as a reminder that the representation was not to be taken literally.[33]

Images of God were later excluded by censorship from the Elizabethan stage, but Shakespeare found several ways to refer to the divine. The word 'God', or, after censorship tightened in 1605, its euphemism 'Heaven', is constantly on the lips of the plays' princes, prelates, and proletarians, in imitation of speech patterns by which people invoke higher power in their daily transactions. God is more real to Shakespeare's characters at moments of private prayer, but only as a projected auditor, never one who answers. Non-biblical gods, such as Juno, Hymen, and Apollo, appear as *dei ex machinis* in some of the comedies. As I will attempt to demonstrate, however, the God of the Bible is actually present in Shakespeare, only disguised as a man or woman.

Theologians postulate that the Judaeo-Christian God is omnipotent and omniscient. But such infinite attributes cannot be conveyed in human terms, so the Bible represents them metaphorically as a finite contrast between superhuman and merely human. God appears as a person who lives on a higher level, possessing power and knowledge that people lack. In his opening speech to Parliament in 1609, King James elaborated some of these metaphors:

Kings are justly called Gods, for that they exercise a manner or resemblance of Divine power upon earth. For if you will consider the attributes to God, you shall see how they agree in the person of a king. God hath power to create, or destroy, make or unmake at his pleasure, to give life, or send death, to judge all and to be judged not, accomptable to none, to raise low things and to make high things low at his pleasure, and to God are both soul and body due. And the like power have kings, they make and unmake their subjects, they have power of raising and casting down of life and of death. Judges over all their subjects, and all causes, and yet accomptable to none but God only. They have power to exalt low things and abase high things, and make of their subjects like men at the Chess, a pawn to take a Bishop or a knight, and to cry up, or down any of their subjects, as they do their money.[34]

This is not just a megalomaniac fantasy of 'playing God', but the conventional wisdom of the period.

The Tempest's Prospero has more godlike attributes than any other Shakespearian character, reflecting that play's uniquely rich connections with the Bible. He is creator and destroyer, like the maker of Eden and the Flood; he is founder of a chosen line, like the God of Abraham, Isaac, and Jacob; he is the deviser of plagues and torments like the God of Exodus and Revelation, and like him the judge at the tribunal where all are brought for sentence. Shakespeare's King Henry V is a man of war and a national leader like the God in the rest of Exodus, and when he experiences fear and is disappointed by his followers, he becomes the sacrificial God of the New Testament. *Measure for Measure*'s Duke Vincentio, whose name means 'the conqueror', is God the judge, who exalts low things and abases the high and makes chess pieces of his subjects as the Bible's God does with Abraham and Job and Christ's disciples.

In the Bible, the relationship between God and people is depicted in terms of hierarchical human relationships: king and subject, parent and child, master and servant, teacher and student. Tensions in such relationships, observed from the viewpoint of the superior, are attributable to the stupidity, rebelliousness, and treachery of the inferior. Since direct instruction does not work, the superior uses a combination of concealment and revelation to teach the inferiors truths they resist. God overhears Adam and Eve in the garden and then interrogates them as if he had not. He tests Abraham and Jacob and Job with tricks and with cruel ordeals whose meaning and motive are hidden from them. He comes to save the world hidden in the person of a poor carpenter and allows himself to be crucified in order to convey a lesson to those who do not follow him and to those who do. Shakespeare's quasi-divine saviours frequently use such disguises. Henry V misleads his father, his bar-room buddies, his treacherous lords, his clergy, his French enemies, and his reluctant bride, before he finally shows his hand. Edgar deceives his father in *King Lear* with a fake exorcism and a false miracle to liberate him from suicidal pessimism. The Friar in *Much Ado About Nothing* rescues a near-tragic situation of misunderstanding with a pious fraud leading to the final moment of revelation.

Shakespeare's most vivid theological metaphors come from the world of the theatre, where the hierarchy of divine and human is richly suggested by relationships between author and character, author and actor, and actor and audience, especially in so far as they involve concealment and revelation. Playwrights have godlike control in casting and controlling actors who recite the lines written for them. But actors also have a divine superiority to the audience because they know the script and can predict what comes next and because they are creating rather than believing in an illusion. Such metaphysical relationships are often explored in Shakespeare's metatheatrical scenes when disguised figures such as Rosalind in *As You Like It* or the Lord in the Induction to *The Taming of the Shrew* establish a vantage point above and beyond that of other characters.

In the Bible, all human characters are created by the authorship of God, but he also watches and judges them as audience and critic. In this sense, the theatregoer, like a member of Theseus' party watching 'Pyramus and Thisbe' in *A Midsummer Night's Dream*, takes a godlike role in relation to the players, since he or she is the one being entertained, doing the judging, and eventually walking out of the playhouse into a larger life after the revels are ended and the 'insubstantial pageant' has 'melted into air, into thin air' (*Tempest*, 4.1.155, 150). An ancient proverb expressed this idea—*totus mundus agit histrionum*—everyone is an actor—and a questionable tradition holds that it was inscribed on the portal of the Globe Theatre. Shakespeare elaborated it in the famous speech beginning 'All the world's a stage, | And all the men and women merely players' (*As You Like It*, 2.7.139–66). A poem of Shakespeare's contemporary Sir Walter Raleigh makes this connection between theatrical and theological perspectives more explicit:

> What is our life? a play of passion
> Our mirth the music of division
> Our mothers' wombs the 'tiring houses be,
> Where we are dressed for this short comedy,
> Heaven the judicious sharp spectator is,
> That sits and marks still who doth act amiss
> Our graves that hide us from the searching sun
> Are like drawn curtains when the play is done
> Thus march we playing to our latest rest
> Only we die in earnest, that's no jest.[35]

To a theatre professional, the Bible's two-tiered reality of God and human provides a practical framework for telling stories.

Most interpretations of the Bible adopt God's point of view, but the text can be viewed through a contrary perspective from which inferior humans appear as victims and the superior deity looks like a tyrant. Outspoken readers from third-century Marcionites to the romantic William Blake to the contemporary Harold Bloom have found the Father God of the Bible to be more of a villain than a hero. Shakespeare's truly malevolent characters, such as Iago or Richard III, are clever theatrical liars who place themselves on a superhuman level over those they trick and control. Even Shakespeare's benevolent God-figures display the vices that go with superior power and knowledge: impatience, self-righteousness, anger, cruelty, jealousy, and pride. It is possible that Shakespeare sometimes regarded his own role of playwright and performer as godlike, his own book as potent and capacious as 'The Book'. He would then probably recognize the Bible God's unappealing traits as his own. Both piety and prudence might convince him to retreat from that role when it felt most alluring, to take off his magician's robe, and drown his book as soon as it was complete.

4

Two inferences follow from the hypothesis that Shakespeare was influenced by the Bible and that he interpreted it freely. One is that understanding the plays' references requires a thorough familiarity with the Scriptures. A second is that these references generate what Bloom calls 'strong' readings—that is, they illuminate fresh and surprising meanings in the biblical text. A modern example of this twofold authorial process is provided by the writer Jane Smiley, whose novel, *A Thousand Acres*, is patterned upon the plot, characters, and themes of *King Lear* though set in modern-day Kansas.[36] The book is comprehensible and engaging to people who do not know Shakespeare's tragedy or its influence, but they are missing a great deal. Smiley's story departs from Shakespeare by filling in a past history of the family that involves the father's sexual abuse of two of his daughters, but that new addition suggests intriguing possibilities about the characters in the earlier play.

The twisting path among meanings that the Bible points to in Shakespeare and that Shakespeare points to in the Bible is marked by allusion. The allusion is the sign at which two meanings intersect, a point of reference where, in Robert Alter's words, an author 'activat[es] an earlier text as part of the new system of meaning and aesthetic value of his own text'.[37] In the alluding later text, the reference may take the form of a verbatim citation of the earlier evoked text. But it may also be a paraphrase or echo. In either alluding or evoked text, the link may apply only to a phrase or globally to the work's overall theme and structure. The alluding text may be consonant with the evoked text's original meanings or it may subvert them by distorting their form and changing its context.

For example, in *Measure for Measure*, Shakespeare's title alludes to a saying of Jesus reported in the gospel of Matthew: 'judge not that ye be not judged. For with what judgement ye judge, ye shall be judged: and with what measure ye mete, it shall be measured to you again' (Matt. 7: 1–2), hinting that the whole play is designed to prove this point and suggesting that its plot runs parallel to the plot of the gospel narrative. In the final moments of the play, the Duke himself alludes to the same passage: 'Like doth quit like, and measure still for measure . . . . We do condemn thee to the very block | Where Claudio stooped to death' (*Measure*, 5.1.408, 411–12). However, he uses the reference to support a command that contradicts the saying of Jesus. Another look at the evoked text turns up a different passage in which Jesus specifically rebuts the sense of the saying employed by the Duke: 'Ye have heard that it hath been said, "An eye for an eye, and a tooth for a tooth." But I say unto you, "Resist not evil: but whosoever shall smite thee on thy right cheek, turn to him the other also" ' (Matt. 5: 38–9). It turns out that the Duke was deliberately misleading the person he addressed with the biblical reference in order to goad her to act on a new-found inner desire to extend mercy to her enemy. The most significant allusion here is not the verbal echoing of the earlier text but a complex network of underlying parallels. The Duke, like the New Testament God, succeeds in governing his people by teaching them to go beyond the letter of the law that they think they have been told, a law that they have foundered upon, whether trying to break or to obey it.

As this example demonstrates, allusion works by hidden meanings, coded communication between author and reader. It requires the reader to be familiar with the absent evoked text and eager to participate in the active process of interpretation. As the Bible itself evolved over thirteen hundred years of accretion and deletion by its own authors and editors, it steadily accumulated more networks of allusion. And for this reason, as Alter observes, 'the Bible has always been the text par excellence to be interpreted, the object of endless homiletical and philological ingenuity, the occasion for codifying whole systems of hermeneutical principles'.[38]

Two traditional principles of scriptural interpretation facilitate the study of Shakespeare and the Bible: typology and midrash. Typology is a method of noting similarities and correspondences between texts. On the basis of those similarities, one thing or event is claimed to stand for or represent another. The ancestor of literary criticism's 'source and analogue' study, typology was used by later biblical writers and commentators to point out how an early event or passage—the type—prefigured and thereby explained and validated a later one—the antitype. They often noted, for example, that the story of the sacrifice of Isaac in Genesis 22 anticipates and stands for the story of God's sacrificing his only son, Jesus. Such typological commentaries referring backwards and forwards, especially between passages of the Old and New Testaments, fill the margins of English Bibles. An example of a typological relation between Shakespeare and the Bible is that between the underdog victory of the Israelite forces over Pharaoh's at the Red Sea recounted in Exodus and the underdog victory of the English forces against the French at the Battle of Agincourt recounted in *Henry V.*

If 'typology' names the Bible's influence on Shakespeare, Shakespeare's commentary on the Bible can be called midrash. 'The Midrash' is a third-century CE collection of rabbinical glosses on passages in the Hebrew Bible.[39] Generically, midrash refers to a technique of interpretation that expands and elaborates the biblical narrative. It derives from the verb 'to study' or 'to search out', and it signifies 'a way of delving more deeply than the literal meaning ... an instrument for imparting contemporary relevance to biblical events'.[40] Midrash unfolds symbolic meanings latent in the scriptural texts with analytical techniques 'linking the various parts of the Bible together by the discovery of typological patterns, verbal echoes, and rhythms of repetition'.[41] The Talmud refers to such analysis as 'a hammer which awakens the slumbering sparks in the rock', for it generates new stories, dense revisions of the original, and more symbolic expressions that warrant further explication.[42]

For example, 'the first midrashic comment on the first word of the Bible ... links that word *bereshit* ("in the beginning") with the word *reshit. Reshit* signifies Wisdom, which is personified in the speaker of Proverbs 8: 22, "God created me as the beginning of his way, the first of his works of old." '[43] In classical Hebrew, 'Wisdom' is also synonymous with Torah, or the Scriptures. The midrash thus discovers the Bible itself within the Hebrew letters of its own beginning, the beginning of the world. The gospel of John begins with a similar midrash on Genesis in Greek: 'In the beginning was the Word ...'. Jesus himself performs midrash when, in response to the disciple's question of why he speaks in parables, he explicates the parable he has just related with yet another parable: 'Hear ye therefore the parable of the sower.

Whensoever a man heareth the word of the kingdom, and under-standeth it not, the evil one cometh, and catcheth away that which was sown in his heart: and this is he which hath received the seed by the wayside' (Matt. 13: 18–19). Shakespeare's *King Lear* performs a mid-rashic elaboration of the book of Job. With plot, characters, and imagery that imitate the scriptural tragedy, the later author provides an explication and commentary on its thematic search for reconcilia-tion between human and God, and a way of 'imparting contemporary relevance to biblical events'.

Midrash has been referred to as 'creative exegesis'.[44] It makes word-play, storytelling, and interpretation come together to liberate pleas-ure, creativity, and knowledge. This is itself the topic of another midrash: 'In the continuation of the passage from Proverbs . . . Torah is pictured as a nursling (or nurse): "Then I was by him as a nursling: and I was daily his delight, playing always before him" (8: 30) . . . God takes his delight with the words of the Torah and men are invited to do the same.'[45] By writing new stories that elaborate and comment play-fully on the Bible's, Shakespeare himself took up the invitation to 'kiss the book'.

5

Typology illuminates patterns of repetition and variation between earlier and later texts that illuminate both. Midrash illuminates an earlier text with elaborations that create a later text typologically related to it. The remainder of this book uses typology to scout out explicit links, as well as echoes, reverberations, and hidden corres-pondences to make sense out of parts of Shakespeare's plays and of the Bible where meaning seems opaque or indeterminate. It also uses midrash, combining wordplay, storytelling, and interpretation to blend typological readings of Shakespeare and the Bible into a composite narrative of its own, a tale with a beginning, middle, and end.

The narrative's architecture is patterned on both the big books it links together. Each of the six chapters following this introduction pairs one book of the Bible with a single Shakespeare play in a sequence that follows scriptural chronology from the beginning of time to its end. The first three deal with books of the Hebrew Bible and the last three with books of the Christian Bible, mirroring the bilateral symmetry remarked upon by many interpreters. *The Tempest* is paired both with the Bible's opening book of Genesis and with its closing book of Revelation, partly because of its double position as the first play in the Folio and the last play Shakespeare wrote in its entirety, and also to highlight 'the typical midrashic predilection for multiple interpretations rather than for a single truth behind the text'.[46] Although only six out of forty-six biblical books and five out of thirty-six Shakespeare plays are fully treated, they make for a representative selection and a coherent sequence.[47] Biblical genres include creation myth, history, wisdom literature, gospel, epistle, and apocalypse. Shakespearian genres include romance, history, tragedy, and comedy.

All six of the succeeding chapters tell their biblical and Shakespearian stories in tandem, emphasizing the typological and midrashic interplay between them. In Chapters 2, 5, and 7, narrative parallels take precedence over thematic ones because in both *The Tempest* and *Measure for Measure* Shakespeare created protagonists consistently modelled upon the Bible's God. Chapters 3, 4, and 6 focus more on thematic parallels that come forward in the absence of a God-figure in the plays. Various critical approaches are brought to bear in every chapter, but each has a different emphasis. The narrative-centred chapters are more formalist, archetypal, and performance-oriented, the thematic ones more concerned with historical contexts of composition and reception.

Consistent with the five-act structure of Shakespeare's plays, each chapter is divided into five parts. In the chapters that follow, these five parts can be roughly correlated with five recurrent concerns: the place of book and play in the larger structure of Bible and Folio; generic elements they share; specific allusions that link them, especially those constructing an image of God; parallels of plot and theme; and significant differences between them.

In Wallace Stevens's poem, 'Peter Quince at the Clavier', a character from Shakespeare's *A Midsummer Night's Dream* muses upon the mutability and permanence of beauty by retelling the biblical story of Susanna and the Elders. During a discussion of that poem in *The Pleasures of Reading*, Robert Alter reflects upon the kind of 'global allusion' this book explores between Shakespeare and the Bible:

The most effective uses of global allusion . . . occur when the introduction of the evoked text is dictated not by arbitrary choice but by a sense on the part of the writer that there is something in the nature of things that requires the allusion . . . . Milton recreates classical epic in *Paradise Lost* in part because he is persuaded of a typological relation of the classical to the biblical . . . . Thus behind many global allusions is a perceived structure of history, an assumed grammar of the imagination that underwrites or even necessitates the wedding of the two texts.[48]

I doubt that Shakespeare intended to marry his book to the Bible, as did Dante, Spenser, Milton, and Blake, but I do think he intended them to embrace.

| 2

Posterity and Prosperity: Genesis in The Tempest

I

The Bible opens with the image of a stormy sea: 'In the beginning God created the heaven and the earth. And the earth was without form and void, and darkness was upon the deep, and the Spirit of God moved upon the waters' (Gen. 1: 1–3). Upon this buzzing, blooming confusion, onomatopoetically called *tōhû wābōhû* in the original Hebrew, the speech of the creator first imposes meaning: the polarities of light and dark, day and night, sea and land. Shakespeare's first words in the First Folio are: 'A tempestuous noise of thunder and lightning heard'. The universe of his plays comes into being as confused and desperate shouts hardly separable from the deafening roar of wind and sea out of which they arise. In the next scene a magical creator appears to give them meaning. The parallel may be accidental, since there is no evidence that Shakespeare himself planned the Folio, but it points to some essential similarities between the book of Genesis and *The Tempest*.

Both are cosmic creation myths, stories of the emergence of complex, articulated being from nothingness or chaos.[1] Just as the Bible's God makes the world he populates and then interacts with it, Prospero conjures up the world of *The Tempest* with his magical utterances and peoples it with his own offspring, along with the demons over whom he has taken control. This is at least strongly suggested when he explains to his daughter that the 'direful spectacle of the wreck' that she and the audience have observed with horror, 'I have with such

THE
TEMPEST.

Actus primus, Scena prima.

A tempestuous noise of Thunder and Lightning heard: Enter a Ship-master, and a Botesswaine.

Master.

Ote-swaine.

Botes. Heere Master: What cheere?

Mast. Good: Speake to th'Mariners: fall too't, yarely, or we run our selues a ground, bestirre, bestirre. *Exit.*

Enter Mariners.

Botes. Heigh my hearts, cheerely, cheerely my harts: yare, yare: Take in the toppe-sale: Tend to th'Masters whistle: Blow till thou burst thy winde, if roome enough.

Enter Alonso, Sebastian, Anthonio, Ferdinando, Gonzalo, and others.

Alon. Good Botesswaine haue care: where's the Master? Play the men.

Botes. I pray now keepe below.

Anth. Where is the Master, Boson?

Botes. Do you not heare him? you marre our labour, Keepe your Cabines: you do assist the storme.

Gonz. Nay, good be patient.

Botes. When the Sea is: hence, what cares these roarers for the name of King? to Cabine; silence: trouble vs not.

Gon. Good, yet remember whom thou hast aboord.

Botes. None that I more loue then my selfe. You are a Counsellor, if you can command these Elements to silence, and worke the peace of the present, wee will not hand a rope more, vse your authoritie: If you cannot, giue thankes you haue liu'd so long, and make your selfe readie in your Cabine for the mischance of the houre, if it so hap. Cheerely good hearts: out of our way I say. *Exit.*

Gon. I haue great comfort from this fellow: methinks he hath no drowning marke vpon him, his complexion is perfect Gallowes: stand fast good Fate to his hanging, make the rope of his destiny our cable, for our owne doth little aduantage: If he be not borne to bee hang'd, our case is miserable. *Exit.*

Enter Boteswaine.

Botes. Downe with the top-Mast: yare, lower, lower, bring her to Try with Maine-course. *A plague—*

A cry within. *Enter Sebastian, Anthonio & Gonzalo.*

vpon this howling: they are lowder then the weather, or our office: yet againe? What do you heere? Shal we giue ore and drowne, haue you a minde to sinke?

Sebas. A poxe o'your throat, you bawling, blasphemous incharitable Dog.

Botes. Worke you then.

Anth. Hang cur, hang, you whoreson insolent Noyse-maker, we are lesse afraid to be drownde, then thou art.

Gonz. I'le warrant him for drowning, though the Ship were no stronger then a Nut-shell, and as leaky as an vnstanched wench.

Botes. Lay her a hold, a hold, set her two courses off to Sea againe, lay her off.

Enter Mariners wet.

Mari. All lost, to prayers, to prayers, all lost.

Botes. What must our mouths be cold?

Gonz. The King, and Prince, at prayers, let's assist them, for our case is as theirs.

Sebas. I'am out of patience.

An. We are meerly cheated of our liues by drunkards, This wide-chopt-rascall, would thou mightst lye drowning the washing of ten Tides.

Gonz. Hee'l be hang'd yet, Though euery drop of water sweare against it, And gape at widst to glut him. *A confused noyse within.* Mercy on vs. We split, we split, Farewell my wife, and children, Farewell brother: we split, we split, we split.

Anth. Let's all sinke with' King

Seb. Let's take leaue of him. *Exit.*

Gonz. Now would I giue a thousand furlongs of Sea, for an Acre of barren ground: Long heath, Browne firrs, any thing; the wills aboue be done, but I would faine dye a dry death. *Exit.*

Scena Secunda.

Enter Prospero and Miranda.

Mira. If by your Art (my deerest father) you haue Put the wild waters in this Rore, alay them: The skye it seemes would powre down stinking pitch, But that the Sea, mounting to th' welkins cheeke, Dashes the fire out. Oh! I haue suffered With those that I saw suffer: A braue vessell

A   (Who provision in mine art | So safely ordered that there is ... not so much perdition as an hair | Betid to any creature in the vessel' (*Tempest*, 1.2.28–31). Not only has the cataclysmic event been completely under his control, but his reassurance is phrased in the words of St Paul: 'For there shall not an hair fall from the head of any of you' (Acts 27: 34), and Jesus: 'all the hairs of your head are numbered: fear not therefore ...' (Luke 12: 7).

Creation myths, like the Big Bang theory, tell of the beginning of time and usually imply its apocalyptic end. Though the notion of a start and finish of time is difficult to imagine in general, it makes clear sense when applied to stories, which are narrative representations of reality structured by beginnings, middles, and endings. In the Bible's last book, where chronicle dissolves into vision, time folds up into eternity. In the Bible's first book, eternity unfolds into time as its stories progress from the opening demarcation of day and night to the creation of matter, life, consciousness, and then, via Adam's dream, to the birth of Eve, the activation of human freedom, and the beginnings of family, society, and history.

The Tempest, whose title signifies storm and time in early modern English,[2] also progresses into temporality from a beginning that is both the timeless chaos of the storm and an Edenic preserve where father and child have remained in idyllic stasis. 'The hour's now come ...', says Prospero, for him to retrieve the story of his past from 'the dark backward and abyss of time' (1.2.37, 50). From then on he continually watches the clock. His daughter's awakening to the temporal process begins with repeated lapses into sleep, but leads to a strong sense of her previous lineage and her future destiny. As they both become involved with the many characters swept up on the shore of their island, their story merges with a historical chronicle of two large ducal dynasties. By the end of both works, as the creation comes to maturity, the extratemporal creators are absorbed into time. God's role as provider, teacher, and governor is passed to the human leader Joseph; Prospero divests himself of magic powers and takes on the mortality he shares with those he has ruled. As time unfolds in a creation myth, so does space. In Genesis the setting expands from the pastoral confines of the Garden of Eden through the Canaanite desert to the epic vistas of the Egyptian empire. In *The Tempest* the setting expands from the domestic compound of Prospero's cell to the island's varied landscapes and then to all of Mediterranean Europe and beyond.

Situated at the beginning of a body of stories, creation myths are seminal. Just as Genesis functions as a seed containing the germinal patterns of most later stories in the Bible, so *The Tempest*, it has often been observed, contains in concentrated form many of the plots and themes of Shakespeare's other Comedies, Histories, and Tragedies. These seminal elements deal directly with fundamental human functions—what Northrop Frye calls 'primary concerns': 'food and drink, along with related bodily needs; sex; property (i.e. money, possessions, shelter, clothing, and everything that constitutes property in the sense of what is "proper" to one's life), liberty of movement. The general object of primary concern is expressed in the biblical phrase "life more abundant".'[3] Another word for this is 'prosperity', cognate with 'Prospero', the name of the protagonist.

The creation at the opening of Genesis leads to an ongoing process of procreation denoted by its cognate word, 'generation'. Generations result from the effects of time, mortality, and continuity, manifested as the ageing and dying of individuals and the passage of their genetic material to children. J. P. Fokkelman observes that the 'overriding concern' of the first book of the Bible is 'life-survival-offspring-fertility-continuity'.[4] Generation is thus linked to family, the seminal cultural institution. The recurrent recording of genealogies in Genesis reflects the theme of family in the accompanying narratives. In fact, the first edition of the King James Bible begins with thirty-four folio pages of genealogical charts tracing lineage from Adam to Christ, while the succession of deaths and births is still recorded on pages inserted into family Bibles. The 'project' that Prospero has long prepared and that he sets in motion at the opening of the play also centres upon founding a chosen family. Like Genesis's God, as the story concludes, he retreats from absolute rule to limited guidance, from creator to procreator, from parent to grandparent, while the next generation advances from children to progenitors. Both God and Prospero bequeath their descendants a promise that temporal evolution is progress, that posterity will inherit prosperity, or 'life more abundant'. But the promise is conditional because the continuity of generation is unpredictable, the outcome not of a preordained plan but of the struggle for existence.

A creation myth represents genesis at several levels. The myth must both contain and be contained by the originating events it records. The creator it describes is prior to the creation, but also part of it, in so far as he is created by the text that describes him. The creator God, therefore, must be both the story's protagonist and its author. In its later passages and commentaries the Bible draws attention to this dimension of its opening. 'In the beginning was the Word', writes John the Evangelist. The first midrashic comment on the first word of Genesis states that God created Wisdom, meaning the Scripture itself, before he made the world. Psalm 139 implies that his book is a script that exists before it is performed: 'Thine eyes did see me, when I was without form: for in thy book were all things written, which in continuance were fashioned, when there was none of them before' (v. 16).

Likewise, there are suggestions that the character Prospero can be construed as the author of the script of *The Tempest* in which he is the subject. It is hinted by his proprietary anxiety about each scene, by his explicit role as author of plays within the play, by his farewell to his book in the last act, and by his direct address to reader and audience in the epilogue. Such identification is a central conception of Peter Greenaway's cinematic midrash on the play, *Prospero's Books*, which intercuts images of turbulent water with images of a quill pen inscribing the first words of the text, and which assigns all the characters' speeches to the voice of Prospero sounding them out as he writes.[5] That this character should be construed both as God and as author seems appropriate to a playwright's playful reflection upon biblical creation.

The process of growth, articulation, and proliferation through time described in Genesis seems to govern its own development as a literary narrative. It begins with the single voice of an author constructing the natural universe in accordance with a simple, preordained plan. But after the creation of human characters in his own image, the story takes on a life of its own. It seems to reproduce itself down the generations from Adam to Joseph, evolving from primal myth into longer, more complex, even novelistic units, as if itself driven by an inner principle of elaboration allowing the future to grow freely and unpredictably like an improvisation out of the past while the author's presence recedes and disappears. The same kind of structural change can be discerned in *The Tempest*, through the increasing length and dramatic complexity of scenes as the play proceeds.

2

Prospero's retrospective exposition of past events in the second scene of *The Tempest* (1.2.1–374) co-ordinates with the section labelled by the editors of the New English Bible as 'The Beginnings of History' (Gen. 2: 5–11: 10) and by the authors of the Geneva Bible's prefatory 'Argument' as the period when 'the wicked . . . falling most horribly from sin to sin . . . provoked God . . . at length to destroy the whole world'. The protagonist and chief speaker in these sections is not the calm and benevolent creator who fashions the world with words but one locked in violent struggle with subjects who rebel and threaten him. The primary concern of these stories is basic survival, which is marginal in the early conditions of a state of nature. This image of the creator may derive from the widely dispersed Near Eastern mythical figure of the conqueror-colonist who first brought the world into being by defeating monsters: 'Thou didst divide the sea by thy power: thou breakest the heads of the dragons in the waters. Thou breakest the head of Leviathan in pieces and gavest him to be meat for the people in wilderness' (Ps. 74: 13–14).

In Genesis God's antagonists are the ambitious Eve who, aligned with the serpent, persuades credulous Adam to eat forbidden fruit; Cain, a jealous and murderous brother; the violent contemporaries of Noah affiliated with offspring of the sons of God and the daughters of men; and the aspiring inhabitants of Babel who want to make a name for themselves by building a tower to heaven. In *The Tempest*, Prospero tells Miranda how his lack of vigilance 'in my false brother | Awaked an evil nature' (1.2.92–3), who then 'new created | The creatures that were mine, I say—or changed 'em | Or else new formed 'em' (1.2.81–3), so that in league with Alonso he took control of the state. Prospero also recalls the island's malignant earlier ruler, Sycorax, and the revolt of her son, Caliban, its primitive inhabitant whose brutish nature he had attempted to elevate until the monster sought to retake control by mating with Prospero's daughter and overthrowing his rule.

The ruler punishes the rebels, indulging a vengeful rage and threatening to undo his own acts of creation with reversions to disorder. God

drives Adam and Eve out of the garden he planted for them into a
barren landscape, he sends Cain wandering, and he returns the cosmos
to chaos with the Flood, a forerunner of other tempests he unleashes
against those he wants to discipline—at the Red Sea (Exod. 14: 21–31),
on the way to Tarsis (Jonah 1: 4–2: 10), at Galilee (Matt. 8: 23–6), and
off the coast of Cyprus (Acts 27: 4–20). He also creates a mental
tempest when he renders the universal human language into a babble
of incomprehensible dialects. Prospero re-establishes his dominance
as 'A god of power' (1.2.10) and 'a prince of power' (l. 54) by throwing
Caliban out of his home, forcing him to live by the sweat of his brow,
and reducing the language that he taught him into profitless cursing,
by repeatedly storming at Ariel that he will be returned to the oak that
imprisoned him, and by tormenting his countrymen with the pro-
longed ordeal of death by drowning.

The horror of that ordeal is vividly conveyed in one of the longest
descriptive passages in the Bible (Gen. 7: 1–24). This horror is relieved
by an equally lively and extended description of the chosen remnant's
salvation, with its anxious waiting, its raven, dove, and olive branch,
and its account of debarkation on to dry land (Gen. 7: 24–8:22). God
seals that experience with a statement of regret and a vow to all living
things never again to send such destruction (Gen. 8: 21) and marks it
with the rainbow to forge a link between heaven and earth (9: 13–14).
Prospero likewise relents and shows his mercy as an agent of deliverance, first to Miranda, in the words cited earlier, eventually to all the
victims of the shipwreck whom he spares from drowning and other
torments, and finally to Ariel and Caliban, whom he frees from
slavery. Upon sparing Ferdinand and Miranda from his rage in the
fourth act, like Noah's God, Prospero presents them with the spectacle
of a rainbow and a blessing of fertility.

3

The Tower of Babel story in ch. 11 marks the end of a major structural
division in the book of Genesis. It corresponds to the shift from
Prospero's narration of past events to the beginning of new activity
that occurs with the entrance of Ferdinand at 1.2.376 in *The Tempest*. In
the next sections of both works, the creator moves partly into the
background, still retaining control, but no longer the only protagonist.

He shows less raw power than in the earlier sections and behaves in a more deliberate, controlled manner. The narrative units change from short, choppy, self-contained stories to an interconnected continuous sequence of events. Rather than creating, destroying, and re-creating by trial and error, the ruler begins to work by breeding, conditioning, and teaching, using longer intervals of time to improve his offspring through the process of evolution. The means of creation changes from magic powers to sexual reproduction. In this section human figures come forward and take on individual, differentiated, and self-motivated character, but the 'primary concern' most emphasized shifts from personal survival to survival of the family through generation.

The stories of the patriarchs Abraham, Isaac, and Jacob, which occupy chs. 11–36 of Genesis, involve both God and human in pro-creating the one family that will bring forth the tribes, the nation, and ultimately the empire of the 'chosen' or genetically selected people whose story is told in the later books of the Hebrew Bible. One method of generation, appropriate to their early herding culture, is inbreeding. God distinguishes his preferred line of descent with a kind of genetic marker: 'I will make thee exceedingly fruitful: yea, Kings shall proceed of thee . . . . thou, and thy seed after thee in their gen-erations . . . shall circumcise the foreskin of your flesh, and it shall be a sign of the covenant between me and you' (Gen. 37: 6, 9, 11). The subsequent stories of the patriarchs centre on the drama of selecting the chosen over the rejected offspring, largely by virtue of consanguin-ity. Isaac's line prevails over Ishmael's, whose mother, Hagar, was of different class and family origin from Sarah, Abraham's stepsister (Gen. 20: 12). Even though he is the younger brother, Jacob is pre-ferred to Esau, an animalistic hairy man who marries a local Hittite woman rather than his own kin. Jacob's mother, Rebekah, steers him northwards to mate with a first cousin, daughter of her brother (Gen. 28: 1–3). And the apparently unrelated story of the massacre of Shechem by the sons of Jacob for the rape of their sister Dinah reinforces a warning against exogamy (Gen. 34).

As Prospero concludes his exposition of past events, he too turns to concerns of breeding. He introduces Caliban, who like Ishmael is the offspring of an ignoble mother with rival matrilineal claims. When the proto-sibling attempted to people 'This isle with Calibans' (1.2.353), Prospero drove him from the family home and put him in bondage.

Following Caliban's suggestion—'She will become thy bed... And bring thee forth brave brood'—Stefano also tries to claim the inheritance: 'I will kill this man. His daughter and I will be king and queen' (3.2.105–8). But Prospero foils this second upstart servant, and, after assurances of the purity of both Miranda's mother and her grandmother, in Prince Ferdinand he finds a scion of close and distinguished lineage, one whose sister Claribel's competing claims of inheritance have been disposed of by marriage to the heathen King of Tunis.

Within the framework of 'primary concerns' defined by the patriarchal project of establishing a familial line, love and romance function like evolutionary sexual selection. Abraham is tough enough to defeat four kings in battle when he first arrives in Canaan (Gen. 14), and Sarah is so beautiful that Pharaoh and King Abimelech court her. The fact that this couple have their first child together in their nineties makes their offspring particularly precious as the distillation of a lifelong love. Stories of love at first sight recur in this section. With Isaac, the lengthy discovery of the beautiful bride occurs through the eyes of Abraham's anonymous servant (Gen. 24: 10–60), but Jacob's first meeting with Rachel at the well evokes the power of physical passion within the framework of family continuity: 'While he [Jacob] talked with [the herdsmen], Rachel also came with her father's sheep, for she kept them. And as soon as Jacob saw Rachel... then came Jacob near, and rolled the stone from the well's mouth, and watered the flock of Laban his mother's brother. And Jacob kissed Rachel, and lifted his voice and wept... then she ran and told her father' (Gen. 29: 9–12).

Ferdinand's first encounter with Miranda produces a heavenly sensation in both of them—'I might call him | A thing divine, for nothing natural | I ever saw so noble.... Most sure the goddess | On whom these airs attend' (1.2.420–2; 424–5)—before the conversation also quickly turns to fathers. These love scenes recall the innocent sexual encounter of Adam and Eve—'Now they were both naked, the man and his wife, but they had no feeling of shame towards one another' (Gen. 2: 25). That first experiment in perfecting humanity set the pattern of triangular tension among parents, child, and spouse: 'that is why a man leaves his father and mother and is united to his wife, and the two become one flesh' (Gen. 2: 24)—thus glossed in the Geneva Bible: 'So that marriage requireth a greater duty of us toward our wives, than otherwise we are bound to show to our parents.' In order to compensate the parent for loss, the children must contain their desires for one another and for children within a framework of obligations to the parents who fostered them. The aged thereby retain some control over the vigorous young and protection from Oedipal threats such as those of Caliban or Stefano. God drives this lesson home with Abraham by demanding Isaac back after they have bonded (Gen: 22). This trick intensifies Abraham's love for his son, it reinforces his fear of God's authority, it reassures the deity that his chosen successor is not a rebel like so many of his predecessors, and it marks God's recognition of human generosity.

In the case of Abraham's grandson Jacob, God challenges him directly only with a brief wrestling bout, but the young man's father-in-law Laban takes over the role of patriarchal tester. After welcoming his nephew with open arms, he too plays with his nephew's emotions, demanding seven years' hard labour for Rachel's hand in marriage and then substituting his older daughter, Leah, in the wedding bed (Gen. 29: 20–8). Jacob works another seven years to get his choice, but Laban cheats him out of the flocks he has rightfully bred for himself. Only by proving that he has the patience and restraint as well as the cleverness, mettle, and generative prowess to overcome these obstacles—including the ability to do his own selective breeding of goats—does Jacob gain his father-in-law's blessing and his right to go home with his beloved to become his nation's founder.

Ferdinand too must yield to his prospective father-in-law. Unlike Caliban, he willingly performs the servile labour of moving logs to acknowledge Prospero's control. This discipline also corrects Ferdinand's premature assumption about his own father's death and his early, easy accession to the throne (1.2.432–3). The spectacle of Ferdinand's suffering causes Miranda to transfer her love from her father to him. Like Rachel, who steals her father's household gods and escapes with Jacob in secret, Miranda repeatedly violates Prospero's precepts (3.1.36–7, 58–9) and takes the initiative to propose marriage herself. Her father also imposes the ordeal to test Ferdinand's commitment, 'lest too light winning | Make the prize light' (1.2.454–5), for a prince who has already 'liked several women' (3.1.43). Like Laban when he catches up with the couple (Gen. 31: 39–41), he expresses concern about the future treatment of his child, and the need for compensation that later surfaces in his shared grieving with Alonso for the daughters they both have lost to sons-in-law (5.1.146–8). Accepting the pain of this loss is a parental test, shared by God with all mothers and fathers in the Bible.

God and Prospero both offer those who successfully pass their qualifying tests—the selected or 'chosen' ones—a vision of the future with a promise of fertility and prosperity as a reward for distinguishing themselves from those who are rejected. Because Abraham has been willing to sacrifice his son, God says: 'Therefore will I surely bless thee, and will greatly multiply thy seed, as the stars of the heaven, and as the sand which is upon the seashore . . . ' (Gen. 22: 17). Jacob's courtship of Rachel is framed by visions at Beth-El: 'The land upon which thou sleepeth, will I give thee and thy seed. And thy seed shall be as the dust of the earth . . . . Israel shall be thy name . . . . Grow, and multiply: a nation and a multitude of nations shall spring of thee' (Gen. 28: 13–14; 35: 10–11). Prospero apologizes for his severe treatment of Ferdinand and offers compensation: 'All thy vexations | Were but my trials of thy love, and thou | Hast strangely stood the test. Here, afore heaven, | I ratify this my rich gift' (4.1.5–8).

The gift is his daughter, but also the vision of deliverance, fertility, and prosperity in the masque, linked by a rainbow to Jacob's ladder and Noah's flood. Following the vision of parental acceptance and bounty, the young men wish to go no further: 'Then Jacob awoke out of his sleep and said, "Surely the Lord is in this place . . . this is none other but the house of God, and this is the gate of heaven"' (Gen. 28: 16–17). Ferdinand says: 'Let me live here ever! | So rare a wondered father and a wise | Makes this place paradise' (4.1.122–4).

The end of Jacob's personal quest arrives when he is renamed Israel, the progenitor of the future nation. His story concludes the patriarchal section of Genesis. From here on God recedes further from his creation, removing himself completely from the narrative as speaker and player and standing outside events as Providence. Though Joseph is the protagonist of the longest story in Genesis, God never addresses him directly. Instead, Joseph becomes a kind of God-human, a stand-in, following his own lights but mysteriously linked to the deity, a brother of other humans, but one who lives on a higher level.

As his daughter and future son-in-law sit enthralled by his wedding gift, Prospero brings his breeding to conclusion. The finale of the masque states his wish for an eternal happy ending for the new couple complete with the banishment of winter and the reconciliation of peasants and demigoddesses. But, before he can join them in dancing with the masquers, they are interrupted by two disturbing realities that keep both the masque itself and the play from reaching closure. With a tempest-like 'hollow and confused noise', Prospero reminds himself that he has unfinished business with the rebellious faction of the clowns and with his brother's conspiracy. That noise also tolls the onset of retirement, old age, and death. While Ferdinand and Miranda take on the world, changed from naïve romantics to chess players who can 'for a score of kingdoms ... wrangle' and still 'call it fair play' (5.1.177–8), he must relinquish it. Coming in a flash, this realization about genesis and generation, fulfilment and completion, nevertheless is disorienting for young and old alike: 'Sir, I am vexed. | Bear with my weakness. My old brain is troubled. | Be not disturbed with my infirmity' (4.1.158–60).

The transformation from creator-god-father to prospective grand-father and corpse leads to Prospero's abjuring his magic, freeing his slave-spirits, and releasing his hold on the humans under his spell. This completion of the Ferdinand and Miranda romance plot in *The Tempest* parallels the silent retreat of God once Jacob has become Israel at the end of the patriarchal chapters of Genesis.

4

Resemblances between Genesis's Joseph and Shakespeare's Prospero are detailed and striking.[6] Linguistically they are linked by the word 'prosperity'—'And the Lord was with Joseph and he was a man that prospered . . . . And his master saw that . . . the Lord made all that he did to prosper in his hand' (Gen. 39: 2–3). Prosperity can emanate from two sources—an external benefactor such as mother earth or father god, or a self-supporting community of people led by an effective leader, first among equals. The process of selection, a zero-sum game, depends on sibling rivalry. The process of co-operation—the strengthening of a 'band of brothers' forming the basis of a nation—must suppress that rivalry. The stories of Joseph and Prospero, the providers, overlap the stories of Joseph and Prospero and their brothers.

In the last section of Genesis the focus of primary concern within the family shifts from paternity, or the relations of parent and child, to fraternity, or the relations between siblings. This shift is predicated upon the disappearance of God, but the theme has been present from the earliest chapters in the stories of Cain and Abel, Abraham and Lot, Isaac and Ishmael, and Jacob and Esau. According to Fokkelman: 'Finally in the last cycle of the book the psychology of crime, guilt, remorse and compunction among brothers is worked out much more thoroughly, under the direction of the master manipulator Joseph . . . the theme of brotherhood, a metonymy for the bond that links humanity, is handled with growing complexity from the beginning of Genesis to the end'.[7]

Prospero is not only a patriarch. His project of breeding optimal progeny shares priority with his project of working out his troubled relationship with his brother, Antonio, and his daughter's future in-law, Alonso. Sibling rivalry—what Hamlet's father calls the 'primal eldest curse'—drives Antonio to plot with Alonso to kill the rightful Duke Prospero and drives Sebastian in turn to plot with Antonio to kill his brother, Alonso, just as Joseph's brothers plot to kill the distinctively robed brother favoured by his father. Resolving sibling rivalry requires somewhat different strategies from resolving generational conflict. The chosen brother, like the parent, first needs to establish dominance, but in order to succeed he must also appear to relinquish it, acknowledging, as Prospero does, that he is not father or god, but 'one of their kind' (5.1.23).

Joseph starts out as 'this dreamer' (Gen. 37: 19), a person with true visions but lacking enough prudence to anticipate the resentment of those who do not share his gifts. Like Prospero, who, 'rapt in secret studies' (1.2.77), 'neglect[s] worldly ends, all dedicated | To closeness and the bettering of my mind' (ll. 89–90), Joseph is at first oblivious to the reality of his political situation. Both he and Prospero 'Awaked an evil nature' (l. 93) in their brothers and, as a result, suffered usurpation, exile, and imprisonment. Joseph's brothers steal him from his father's favour, plan to kill him, and end up imprisoning him in a pit and then selling him into slavery and exile in Egypt. Prospero's brother and his cronies remove him from his dukedom, try to kill him, and allow him to be abandoned at sea in a leaky boat that ends up marooned on the island.

Rudely awakened from innocence and forced to cope for survival in their places of exile, both Joseph and Prospero learn some practical wisdom. As a convict in Pharaoh's gaol, Joseph goes from a dreamer to an interpreter of dreams, using his intelligence as well as his intuition. Though he insists that interpretative power comes from God (Gen. 40: 8), in proclaiming that Pharaoh's two dreams of the fat sheaves and cows being devoured by the lean are really one (43: 25), he uses human analytical skills to penetrate surfaces by discovering abstractions. By predicting that lean years will consume fat ones, he expresses the homespun foresight of the ant to the grasshopper. Prospero has fewer books after his sea voyage, those discreetly selected for him by his counsellor Gonzalo, and, once outside the precincts of his library, he finds enough applicable information in those to gain control over his environment.

Wearing his robe and consulting his books, Prospero teaches the ignorant Caliban to speak and releases Ariel from imprisonment. At the same time he subdues and enslaves them and their fellow native spirits, appropriating their power to rule the elements. After Joseph bests Pharaoh's magicians and sages (Gen. 41: 8), he is entrusted to rule over all Egypt. Dressed in fine clothing and signet ring, he delivers the people from hunger while divesting them of their wealth. By the time fate—in the form of famine and storm—lands their lost brothers in their places of exile, both have exercised their acumen long enough to have risen to the status of 'Prince of Power'.

Having attained power, each pursues the god-human's fraternal initiative to right wrong with vengeance, instruction, and forgiveness. Jacob's sons arrive in Joseph's Egypt desperate for grain and disoriented by travel. Prospero's brother and his companions wander the island waterlogged, bereaved, and exhausted. Both parties have been partially rescued by the exiled brother and find themselves at his mercy—that is, within his power. One source of that power is immediate knowledge. He recognizes them because he remembers the wrong done to him. They do not know him because he is disguised or invisible, but also because they have repressed the memory of their crimes long past.

After harshly accusing the ones he spies on of being spies (Gen. 42: 9; *Tempest*, 1.2.456), the hidden brother manipulates the others into a replay of their earlier crimes of conspiracy and rebellion, now within his control. Joseph insists they return home and bring him their brother Benjamin, who has stayed behind, thereby once again stealing a youngest preferred son away from their father. He does this, one may infer, to enjoy the revenge of inflicting pain on them, and to determine whether they have spared his mother's other son and are capable of repentance. If so, re-enacting the old crime can remind them of what they have forgotten and teach them about the pain it inflicted. Prospero similarly works on the lords by setting up a situation in which the treasonous coup that exiled him is now re-enacted by Antonio and Sebastian against his brother, King Alonso. The pain of being betrayed by his own brother—though only half-conscious—and of apparently losing a son awakens Alonso's memory of having betrayed his brother monarch.

In a comic replay of another element of their crime—selling him for silver and sneaking him into the caravan of the Midianites—Joseph tricks his brothers with an apparent gift of silver in their bags—which will then serve as false evidence of theft. Both elements of this trick recur in *The Tempest*'s subplot of Caliban and the clowns, who are first manipulated into hatching a new conspiracy to overthrow Prospero to gain wealth and power and then entrapped with the false delights of a ducal wardrobe.

Joseph's methods of interrogation activate his brothers' consciences and soon elicit a confession that he overhears: 'And they said one to another, "We have verily sinned against our brother, in that we saw the anguish of his soul, when he besought us, and we would not hear him: therefore is this trouble come upon us"' (Gen. 42: 21). This encourages him to take the cat-and-mouse game further with what may be termed a 'banquet trick'. When the brothers return to Egypt with Benjamin as hostage a few years later, he offers them a resplendent meal, and, while their defences are lowered, he hides a silver goblet in Benjamin's pack. After they depart, 'Joseph said to his steward, "Up, follow after the men and when thou dost overtake them, say unto them, 'Wherefore have ye rewarded evil for good?'"' (Gen. 44: 4). When the packs are opened, Benjamin's is found to contain the goblet, and he and his brothers must return to Joseph, who accuses him of the theft and threatens to keep him as a slave. Similarly, Prospero surprises the hungry nobles with a lavish buffet after having had them led blindly around the island in search of the King's lost son. Watching their approach to the meal from an invisible vantage point above, he arranges for Ariel to spoil the dinner and to deliver a tirade expressing

nough,& drunke
of the beſt wine.

k and had of the beſt drinke with him.

C H A P. XLIIII.

15 *Joſeph accuſeth his brother of theft. 33 Iudah offereth himſelfe to be ſeruant for Beniamin.*

A Fterward he commanded his ſteward, ſaying, Fill the mens ſackes with foode, as much as they can carry, and put euery mans money in his ſackes mouth.

a We may not by this example vſe any vnlawfull practiſes, ſeeing God hath comm̄ā- ded vs to walke in ſimplicitie.

2 And a put my cup, *J meane* the ſiluer cup, in the ſackes mouth of the yongeſt, and his corne money. And he did according to the commande- ment that Ioſeph gaue *him.*

† *Ebr. the morning ſhone.*

3 And in the † morning the men were ſent

3. Text and annotation of the first verses in chapter 44 of Genesis, from the Geneva Bible of 1587

Prospero's wrath, exposing the lords' original guilt, threatening eternal perdition, and demanding full contrition.

The Geneva editors take pains to point out that Joseph's methods are not to be imitated: 'This dissembling is not be followed, nor any particular facts of the fathers not approved by God's word' (gloss to 42: 7). 'We may not by this example use any unlawful practices, seeing God hath commanded us to walk in simplicity' (gloss to 44: 2). Nevertheless, this device produces the desired effect of repentance in both stories. Joseph's oldest brother Judah is willing to sacrifice himself for the release of Benjamin: 'Now therefore, I pray thee, let me thy servant bid for the child, as a servant to my lord, and let the child go up with his brethren. For how can I go up to my father, if the child be not with me, unless I would see the evil that shall come upon my father?' (Gen. 44: 33–4). Alonso falls to the ground acknowledging his crime and willing to give up his own life to return the life of the son that he believes has been taken from him as punishment:

> The winds did sing it to me, and the thunder,
>   . . . pronounced
> The name of Prosper. It did bass my trespass.
> Therefor my son i'th' ooze is bedded, and

> I'll seek him deeper than e'er plummet sounded,
> And with him there lie mudded.
>
> (3.3.96–102)

At this turning-point in both stories the focus shifts to the hidden controlling brother. Each has forced his antagonists to experience the suffering of the victim of fratricide. Each now feels compassion for the repentant criminals. After dismissing his servants, for the moment abjuring his royal powers and distance, Joseph breaks down crying, discloses himself to his brothers' wonderment, forgives them fully, and arranges for them and his father to take up residence in Egypt, where they will be reunited and provided with land and wealth. So too, after Alonso's repentance, Prospero acknowledges his common humanity with those he has dominated and offers them forgiveness:

> shall not myself,
> One of their kind, that relish all as sharply
> Passion as they, be kindlier moved than thou art?
> Though with their high wrongs I am struck to th' quick,
> Yet with my nobler reason 'gainst my fury
> Do I take part. The rarer action is
> In virtue than in vengeance. They being penitent,
> The sole drift of my purpose doth extend
> Not a frown further.
>
> (5.1.22–30)

At the final moment, even Caliban is transformed in Prospero's designation from an 'abhorrèd slave' who will 'any print of good-ness... not take' (1.2.354–5) to a 'thing of darkness I | Acknowledge mine' (5.1.278–9). Once so acknowledged, Caliban too repents, with a word that asks forgiveness and favour, both human and divine: 'I'll be wise hereafter, | And seek for grace' (ll. 298–9).

These revelations, recognitions, restorations, and reconciliations produce an ecstatic happy ending. They also produce a retrospective vindication of all previous confusion and suffering as purposeful contributions to the positive outcome—a theological assertion of the fortunate fall: 'Now therefore be not sad... that he sold me hither: for God did send me before you for your purification... to preserve your posterity in this land, and to save you alive by a great deliverance' (Gen. 45: 5–7), says Joseph. Gonzalo concludes,

> Was Milan thrust from Milan, that his issue
> Should become kings of Naples? O rejoice
> Beyond a common joy! And set it down
> With gold on lasting pillars: in one voyage
> Did Claribel her husband find at Tunis,
> And Ferdinand her brother found a wife
> Where he himself was lost; Prospero his dukedom
> In a poor isle; and all of us ourselves,
> When no man was his own.
>
> (5.1.208–16)

5

Shakespeare liked to write deflating parodies of his own grandiose productions, as, for instance, in *A Midsummer Night's Dream*, where the rude mechanicals' rendition of 'Pyramus and Thisbe' parodies *Romeo and Juliet*. In *The Tempest*, the clown scenes parody the archetypal cosmic creation myths of the Prospero plot as well as its biblical source. Act 2, Scene 2 begins again with the unformed chaos of a storm dissolving the borders between classes—'Misery acquaints a man with strange bedfellows' (1. 39)—as well as between species and individuals: 'This is some monster of the isle with four legs' (1. 65). The drunken butler Stefano gives coherent shape to the chaos as well as healing deliverance with the magic brew stored up in his homemade bark bottle: 'Here is that which will give language to you, cat. Open your mouth. This will shake your shaking' (ll. 82–4). After figuratively bringing Trinculo into the world from under the gabardine, he accepts the worship of Caliban, 'a most poor credulous monster', whose visions of divinity are inspired by the colonizer's firewater: 'That's a brave god, and bears celestial liquor. | I will kneel to him' (ll. 115–16). 'Kiss the book', says Stefano repeatedly, referring to the ritual of swearing by the Bible as he commands the native inhabitant's worship by bottle feeding him dry sherry, profanely suggesting an analogy between it and communion wine or Holy Writ.

Shakespeare translates the mythic discourse of the Bible into still another register, following the lead of Genesis itself. Moving further into time as the stories unfold, its final narrative fills in many particulars of the Egyptian setting, especially of economics and government. The idealistic celebration of the founding of a nation is an appropriate mythic conclusion for a political text. But the authors of Genesis, like the author of *The Tempest*, also observed history through a more materialistic historian's eyes, following the trail of the money and the power.

After the recognition-redemption scene and the Pharaoh's welcome of Jacob to Egypt, the earlier story (Gen. 41: 46–57) of Joseph's deliverance of the land during the lean years by distributing grain stored during the fat ones is repeated. But this time the account is more detailed, plausible, and ironic. Having accumulated a huge surplus by taxing the peasants during the period of glut, Joseph sells it back to them during the famine—first for all their silver, then for their herds. Finally,

> they came unto him the next year, and said unto him, 'We will not hide from my lord, that since our money is spent, and my lord hath the herds of the cattle, there is nothing left in the sight of my lord, but our bodies and our ground . . . Buy us and our land for bread, and we and our land will be bound to Pharaoh: therefore give us seed, that we may live and not die, and that the land go not to waste.' So Joseph bought all the land of Egypt for Pharaoh . . . And he removed the people unto the cities, from one side of Egypt even to the other.
>
> (Gen. 47: 18–21)

The Geneva gloss gives a benevolent appearance to this policy. 'By this changing they signified that they had nothing of their own, but received all of the King's liberality.' But the text makes clear that Joseph's ruthless transformation of Egypt from a feudal to a mercantile society makes it possible for his descendants to expand their numbers at a rate that could never have been supported by the nomadic subsistence conditions they had lived under in Canaan. His centralization of authority also guarantees the privileges now granted by the Pharaoh, at least for the foreseeable future.

The last chapter of Genesis contains an equally cynical rerun of the earlier story of fraternal reconciliation:

> And when Joseph's brethren saw that their father was dead, they said, 'It may be that Joseph will hate us, and will pay us again all the evil, which we did unto him.' Therefore they sent unto Joseph, saying, 'Thy father commanded before his death saying, "Thus shall ye say unto Joseph, forgive now I pray thee, the trespass of thy brethren and their sin: for they rewarded thee evil." And now, we pray thee, forgive the trespass of the servants of thy father's God . . .'. To

whom Joseph said, 'Fear not: for am not I under God? When ye thought evil against me, God dispoiled it to good, that he might bring to pass, as it is this day, and save much people alive. Fear not now therefore, I will nourish you, and your children...' (Gen. 50: 15–21)

Given their persistent mistrust and the narrator's tacit but unmistakable disclosure of their bad faith, and given Joseph's canny strategy towards the Egyptians, this repetition of forgiveness might well be uttered with a touch of irony as well as threat.

The final reconciliation in *The Tempest* is similarly qualified. Apart from all the celebration stand Antonio and Sebastian. These unregenerate schemers never apologize, and retain their witty cynicism to the last. In his final judgement scene, Prospero distinguishes 'holy Gonzalo | Honourable man... a loyal sir' (5.1.62–9) from the forgetful and frail Alonso, who is capable of contrition, and from Antonio, 'most wicked sir, whom to call brother | Would even infect my mouth...' (ll. 132–3). Though he forgives them all, he recognizes that there are people in whom self-interest, cruelty, and power-hunger remain ineradicable. His forgiveness of Antonio involves no expectation of redemption or improvement. He, and others like him, must be continually watched and controlled with tactics that appeal to their limited motives.

Before he relinquishes political power, Prospero appropriately greets each of these three: he embraces Gonzalo, he commiserates with Alonso, and he frightens Antonio with a crafty display of force and fraud:

> Welcome, my friends all.
> But you, my brace of lords, were I so minded,
> I here could pluck his highness' frown upon you
> And justify you traitors. At this time
> I will tell no tales.
>
> .   .   .   .   .
>
>   I do forgive
> Thy rankest fault, all of them, and require
> My dukedom of thee, which perforce I know
> Thou must restore.
>
> (5.1.127–31, 133–6)

By retaining the threat to expose their conspiracy to Alonso, he keeps them in his debt, and, as a result of marrying his daughter to the prince of Naples, 'his death will remove Antonio's last link with the ducal power'.[8] 'The devil speaks in him' (l. 131) says Sebastian.

Political realism goes together with the prophetic vision of an expanded community tracing itself to an originating family. The nation of Italy, which Prospero foresees through the union of his daughter and Alonso's son, is analogous to the nation of Israel envisioned by Joseph and Jacob on the father's deathbed. Jacob's benediction of his progeny is shadowed by power struggles which surface at the moment of blessing, as the son unsuccessfully tries to control his father's determination of precedence among his grandsons, Manasseh and Ephraim (Gen. 48: 17–20). The grandfather's projection of their return to the promised land is filled with predictions of war and fraternal strife. Prospero promises 'calm seas, auspicious gales' for the voyage home (5.1.318), but it is clear that the new kingdom will experience continuing tensions, not only between aristocratic factions, but also as a result of the class hatred between courtiers and mariners. This is loudly voiced by good Gonzalo—whose imagined commonwealth knew no 'riches, poverty, | And use of service' (2.1.156–7)—both at the moment of death in the first scene's storm, and at the concluding moment of miraculous resurrection: 'O look, sir, look, sir, here is more of us! | I prophesied if a gallows were on land | This fellow could not drown' (5.1.219–21). As is appropriate for works that stand at the beginning, the endings of Genesis and *The Tempest* introduce a continuing history, the genre of discourse in which time bears absolute sway.

Historical Types: Moses, David, and Henry V

I

The book of Genesis concludes with Jacob's twelve sons, the children of Israel, established in Egypt and a prophecy that they will eventually multiply into twelve tribes. The book of Exodus begins by reporting that the Egyptians respond to this population explosion with harsh measures: they place the Israelites in bondage and then kill their first sons. The rest of Exodus recounts what follows—the transformation of the Israelites from an enslaved, oppressed, and landless people into a free nation of nomadic warriors poised to conquer the territory of Canaan and claim it as their divinely promised homeland. The narrative conventions of Exodus are no longer those of the mythic, legendary, and novelistic stories of Genesis but those of a national history. In retrospect, the evolutionary pageant of the Bible's first book becomes a prehistorical background for the emergence of a powerful nation-state.

While Exodus is the second of the 'Five Books of Moses'—in Hebrew, 'Torah'; in Greek, 'Pentateuch'—it is the beginning of what has come to be called the Bible's 'Deuteronomic History', a sequence of books extending through Numbers and Deuteronomy to Joshua, Judges, Samuel, and Kings. This history covers the thousand-year-long chronicle of Israel's liberation from slavery, its wandering in the desert, its victories over the native Canaanites, its rivalries among competing tribes, and its establishment of a theocracy, a monarchy, and an empire that triumphs, declines, and is destroyed by its Assyrian and Babylonian rivals. The First Folio collection of Shakespeare's plays also creates a separate division for 'Histories'. It includes ten plays that Shakespeare wrote at different stages of his career, but which later editors, like those of Deuteronomic History, compiled into a single chronological sequence relating a centuries-long succession of events culminating in the birth of Queen Elizabeth.

2

The Deuteronomic narrative itself evolved out of a multitude of competing documentary strains selected and combined by generations of editors before it was canonized into a stable text. According to historical scholars, it was first written down during the reign of the Davidic King Josiah (640–609 BCE) as a repository of Jewish national heritage crafted to unify the rival tribal alliances of Israel and Judah by memorializing common trials and triumphs. Thus, it functioned to define the culture and strengthen the authority of the monarchy.[1] This history also served the interest of the Jerusalem priesthood by placing secular events such as battles, migrations, rebellions, and the selection of leaders within the framework of a turbulent relationship between the Israelites' God and his prophets, kings, and chosen people—his 'kingdom of priests' (Exod. 19: 6). The Deuteronomic History projects a providential pattern on the past. When the Israelites pleased God with strict adherence to ethical righteousness, ritual practice, and avoidance of rival religious cults, they were rewarded by his miraculous interventions. When they displeased him, he arranged for their defeat—by enemy forces, internal dissension, or natural disaster.

Following the perennial tendency of the British to identify them-selves with the Israelites, Shakespeare's sources, Holinshed and Halle, modelled English history on the Bible's providential pattern. They arranged their accounts to teach didactic lessons known collectively as the Tudor myth. In their telling, the succession of events demon-strated God's involvement on the side of the legitimate authorities of State and Church. Rebellion was punished with civil strife, the weak-ening of the nation, and consequent universal suffering. God also punished tyrannical or impious behaviour on the part of leaders by causing their fall, but history taught that disobedience of any sort would bring down divine retribution.

Shakespeare's earliest cycle of history plays written between 1590 and 1593, *Henry VI, Parts 1, 2, and 3*, and *Richard III*, arranges its account of the civil wars between the houses of Lancaster and York with the biblical pattern of God's 'visiting the wickedness of the fathers upon the children, in the third and fourth generation' (Num. 14: 18). The punishment for usurping the throne of Richard II reaches a climax in the tyrannical reign of Richard III, a satanic agent of divine vengeance, who is himself finally defeated in a holy war by the first Tudor monarch, Henry VII, Earl of Richmond. That triumph is celebrated with the declaration, 'Now civil wounds are stopped, peace lives again: | That she may long live here, God say "amen"' (5.8.40–1). Much of the play's plot and language is based on the book of Revelation's account of the battles between the devil and his allies and the triumphant forces of Christ.

The same providential model of English history influences Shakespeare's second tetralogy of history plays written between 1594 and 1599. King Richard, like Saul in the Books of Samuel, is punished for failing to rule properly by the accession of his rival, Henry Bolingbroke. Bolingbroke, now Henry IV, is himself punished for rebellion and dies after a troublesome and guilt-ridden reign. In the last play of this cycle, *Henry V*, the guilt is temporarily suspended while young King Henry V appears as God's chosen warrior against foreign antagonists, the French. His victory is partially modelled upon David's over Goliath. But the extended type or pattern of Henry's story is found earlier, in Exodus. The two hymns he orders to be sung at the news of his victory at Agincourt—the 'Non Nobis' and the 'Te Deum'—derive from verses in the Psalms that celebrate the defeat of the Egyptian armies and God's deliverance of Israel at the Red Sea. They appear midway in the liturgical sequence known as the Egyptian Hallelujah extending from Psalm 113 to 118, a sequence that Jesus and the disciples sang during the Passover celebration at the Last Supper and that Jews still recite at all their great festivals. Holinshed refers to the hymn not as 'Non Nobis' but by the title of Psalm 114, 'In exitu Israel de Aegypto' ('When Israel came out of Egypt').

The miraculous military victory commemorated in the 'Non Nobis' is the core event of salvation in the Bible, the model of all God's interventions in human history. That event is recalled and re-created in other psalms; in accounts of military victories such as Joshua's,

The red Sea. **Exo**

In this figure foure chiefe poyntes are to be considerd. First, that the Church of God is euer subiect in this worlde to the Crosse, and to be afflicted after one sort or other. The second, that the ministers of God following their vocation, shalbe euill spoken of, and murmured against, euen of them that pretende the same cause and religion that they doe. The third, that God deliuereth not his Church incontinently out of dangers, but to exercise their faith and patience continueth their troubles, yea and often times augmenteth them: as the Israelites were nowe in lesse hope of their liues, then when they were in Egypt. The fourth poynt is, that when the dangers are most great, then Gods helpe is most ready to succour: for the Israelites had on either side them, huge rockes and mountaines, before them the Sea, behinde them most cruell enemies, so that there was no way left to escape to mans iudgement.

4. The Israelites about to cross the Red Sea, from the Geneva Bible: this woodcut appears both on the title-pages and, with lengthy caption, at Exodus 14:14 (reproduced here)

David's, the Maccabees', and the archangel Michael's; and in stories of rescue from drowning such as Noah's, Jonah's, and Paul's. In the Geneva Bible, the engraving picturing the Israelites threatened by the Egyptian army at the Red Sea that appears at ch. 14 of Exodus also appears on the title-page of the Old Testament and again on the title-page of the New Testament. The original source of these tales of deliverance is found in what has been identified as the earliest biblical text, 'The Song of the Sea': 'I will sing unto the Lord: for he hath triumphed gloriously... The Lord is a man of war, his name is Jehovah. Pharaoh's chariots and his host hath he cast into the sea. Thy right hand, Lord, is glorious in power: thy right hand, Lord, hath bruised the enemy' (Exod. 15: 1, 3–4). Like the American national anthem, which memorializes a battle during the war of 1812, this song defines national identity by commemorating a miraculous underdog military victory.

The place of the Agincourt story in Shakespeare's English history cycle resembles the place of the Red Sea battle in the Bible: it fixes the central moment both remembered and prefigured. Agincourt elevates Henry into a national hero like Moses, but more importantly it testifies to the intervention of God on our side: 'O God, thy arm was here, | And not to us, but to thy arm alone | Ascribe we all.... Take it God, | For it is none but thine' (*Henry V*, 4.8.106–12), says Henry, once again quoting Scripture: 'For they inherited not the land by their own sword, neither did their own arm save them. But thy right hand, and thine arm...' (Ps. 44: 3). Under penalty of death, all the euphoria and relief of victory must be channelled towards God: 'And be it death proclaimèd through our host | To boast of this, or take that praise from God | Which is his only' (4.8.114–16).

Henry is known as both the most religious and the most warlike of English kings. The Archbishop asserts that 'God and his angels guard your sacred throne' (1.2.7). As opposed to the French who use God's name only to swear, Henry continually invokes his help and blessing. Alone in prayer, he addresses his deity as 'God of battles' (4.1.286). In the Hebrew Bible, God is referred to more than fifty times with the formula, 'Yahweh Sabaoth', the Lord of Hosts. This title was derived from earlier Canaanite and Babylonian deities, who were described as leaders of battalions of followers warring against enemy gods or monsters to bring forth creation. Biblical usage of 'Lord of Hosts' at some times refers to God at the forefront of troops of angels and at others as the chief of the armies of the Israelites. Yahweh's war-god manifestations range from miraculous interventions as a destroyer of Israel's enemies to mundane advice on logistical procedures. Conversely, the human leader of Israel's armies is often equated with a war-god. This is the image of Moses that we are left with by the narrator at the conclusion of the Torah: 'that mighty hand and all that great fear, which Moses wrought in the sight of Israel' (Deut. 34: 12). In Deuteronomy, Moses' voice is often indistinguishable from Yahweh's:

If ye shall hearken therefore unto my commandments, which I command you this day, that ye love the Lord your God and fear him with all your heart, and with all your soul, I also will give rain unto your land in due time, the first rain and the latter, that thou mayest gather in thy wheat, and thy wine, and thine oil. Also I will seed grass in thy fields for thy cattle. (Deut. 11: 13–15)

Patrick Miller labels this underlying biblical principle 'synergism':

at the centre of Israel's warfare was the unyielding conviction that victory was the result of a fusion of divine and human activity... while might of arms and numbers were not the determining factors.... It was yet possible for the people to see themselves as going to the aid of Yahweh in battle (Judg. 5: 23). Yahweh fought for Israel even as Israel fought for Yahweh.... Yahweh was general of both the earthly and the heavenly hosts.[2]

Shakespeare's opening chorus proclaims this conflation of god, king, and general in a blithely syncretic mixture: 'Then should the warlike Harry, like himself, | Assume the port of Mars, and at his heels, | Leashed in like hounds, should famine, sword, and fire | Crouch for employment' (1.0.5–8).

The chorus specializes in such rhetoric of deification, referring to Henry as 'the mirror of all Christian kings' (2.0.6) and instructing us to 'cry, "Praise and glory on his head!"' (4.0.31). Exeter employs similar hyperbole when he warns the French king of Harry's approach, 'in fierce tempest is he coming, | In thunder and in earthquake, like a Jove...' (2.4.99–100). Mixing pagan and biblical references to a storm god, Exeter here alludes to the Yahweh of Ps. 29: 3 and 5: 'The voice of the Lord is upon the waters: the God of glory maketh it to thunder... The voice of the Lord breaketh the cedars...' And in the wording of Henry's battle-cry itself, the ancient biblical identification of God and man returns: 'God for Harry! England and St George!' (3.1.34).

Henry's later exhortations to his beleaguered troops on the morning of the final battle are based on a different rhetorical model in Exodus—one addressed both to the audience within the text and to later listeners and readers. Promising victory to the frightened Israelites on the night before their departure from Egypt, Moses delivers instructions for celebrating this as a feast day with a blood sacrifice and a shared meal that is to protect, mark, and bond them: 'Let every man take unto him a lamb according to the house of the fathers... then all the multitude of the Congregation of Israel shall kill it at even. After they shall take the blood and strike it on the two poles, and on the upper doorpost of the houses where they shall eat it' (Exod. 12: 3, 6–8). Henry proclaims, 'This day is called the Feast of Crispian' (4.3.40) and 'he today that sheds his blood with me | Shall be my brother; be he ne'er so vile, | This day shall gentle his condition' (4.3.61–3). Both speeches prophesy the participation of future generations in the forthcoming events by incorporating instructions for ritual commemoration of them even before they happen. Thus Moses, 'And this day shall be unto you a remembrance: and ye shall keep it an holy feast unto the Lord, throughout your generations . . . for that same day I will bring your armies out of the land of Egypt' (Exod. 12: 14, 17). And thus Henry,

> He that shall see this day, and live t'old age
> Will yearly on the vigil feast his neighbours
> And say, 'Tomorrow is Saint Crispian.'
> Then will he strip his sleeve and show his scars
>
> .   .   .   .   .
>
> Then shall our names
>
> .   .   .   .   .
>
> Be in their flowing cups freshly remembered.
>
> (4.3.44–51, 55)

Though embedded within their historical narratives, both speeches explain future ritual repetitions with reference to the tale that is about to unfold. Moses says, 'And when your children ask you, "What service is this ye keep?" Then ye shall say, "It is the sacrifice of the Lord's Passover, which passed over the houses of the children of Israel in Egypt, when he smote the Egyptians, and preserved our houses." Then the people bowed themselves and worshipped' (Exod. 12: 26–7). And Henry commands, 'This story shall the good man teach his son, | And Crispin Crispian shall ne'er go by | From this day to the ending of the world | But we in it shall be rememberèd' (4.3.56–9). Such breaks of the narrative frame—frequently repeated in the biblical accounts of Exodus—anticipate what is to come, both within the stories themselves and in their later reception.

These anticipations recursively include the audience as participants in past actions, while at the same time instructing them how to make those actions come to pass in the present and stay alive in the future through imaginative re-enactment. The same functions are carried out by Shakespeare's Chorus in its urgent direct addresses to the audience. The Chorus insists that collaboration between author and audience 'in the quick forge and working-house of thought' (5.0.23) is required to make the illusion real, thereby suspending disbelief, and suggesting that providential history is a work of the imagination rather than a transmission of fact.

3

From the early sixteenth century onwards, the providential theory of history was supplemented by a secular humanist approach, what might be called the political theory of history. After studying the classical historians Livy, Tacitus, and Thucydides, Continental historians such as Guicciardini, Bodin, and Machiavelli searched for empirical patterns of causality in stories of the past and discovered them in factors such as geography, technology, class, and crowd psychology. Machiavelli found the Bible interesting not so much as a record of God's plan or as a spiritual guide, but rather as an archive of information about the development of the ancient Israelite state, about resistance and rule, about the behaviour of kings, generals, and armies, and about the influence of religion in politics. To him, Moses appeared as a great founding figure, both of a new state and a new religion, one who succeeded not because he was chosen by God, but because he was a great leader who developed the human ability to make the most of circumstances.[3] In Shakespeare's first history tetralogy, policy and piety are polarized. There the villain Richard Gloucester boasts he will 'set the murderous Machiavel to school' (*3 Henry VI*, 3.2.193). But from the political and religious perspective of the second tetralogy, Machiavelli is affirmed though not acknowledged.

Immediately following the Chorus's invocation of Henry's divine mission at the opening of the play, the audience is made to eavesdrop on a backroom conversation revealing that Henry has secured the Archbishop's sanction for the invasion of France in return for the King's agreement to block the bill in Commons that would force the Church to pay taxes to support the sick and indigent. And though the King insists that the victory of Agincourt is not his but God's, Shakespeare's depiction of Henry and of the way events unfold suggests otherwise. Henry follows his father Bolingbroke's footsteps in thinking and behaving as if the outcome of events is decided by his own courage and cleverness. The elder Henry plans a holy war against the Turks as a means to quell civil war at home and to ease his conscience for usurping the throne, and his dying words include the advice to his son to 'busy giddy minds | With foreign quarrels' to solidify his shaky regime (*2 Henry IV*, 4.3.342–3). Divine purpose and national destiny are shown to be illusions masking a combination of chance and the struggle for power.

In the book of Exodus, Machiavelli found an astute account of the challenges faced by leaders who seek to establish new states or regimes. In order to carry out his destiny, Moses must defeat enemies and maintain unity and support among followers. This is foreshadowed in the biblical story of his killing the Egyptian taskmaster who was beating a Hebrew slave (Exod. 2: 11–14). Next day, when Moses returns to try to get two Hebrews to stop fighting each other, they deny his authority and ask whether he plans to kill them as well. The only way that Moses can take control to achieve God's purpose of forming a nation strong enough to beat the Egyptians and conquer their own territory is by producing belief. In enemies such belief is credibility. In followers it is faith. This is also the task of Henry the Fifth as he takes the throne of an England verging on civil war and reluctant to accept his rule.

One means of producing belief is to supply legal justification for the appropriation of territory. This is provided to the Hebrews by the contractual agreement Moses reports that God made with their fore-father Abraham to grant his seed the promised land. The Archbishop provides Henry with a similar covenant in 'the Law Salique', which 'proves' that he can 'with right and conscience make this claim' (*Henry V*, 1.2.96) to the territory of France. The book of Numbers, the only biblical book explicitly mentioned by Shakespeare, provides support for their interpretation of the law. But such legal justification is largely for home consumption since it is unlikely to persuade those who at present occupy the land.

The next means of producing belief—that of intimidation—is addressed equally to followers and opponents. Threats must be rendered convincing with terror tactics, both to weaken enemy morale and to buttress the confidence of one's own side. God tells Moses to punish Pharaoh with plague after plague to demonstrate the strength of the Israelites, and he repeatedly hardens Pharoah's heart to make him responsible for the suffering of his own people: 'Then there shall be a great cry throughout all the land of Egypt, such as was never none like, nor shall be. But against none of the children of Israel shall a dog move his tongue, neither against man nor beast, that ye may know that the Lord putteth difference between the Egyptians and Israel' (Exod. 11: 6–7). After justification, Henry also resorts to intimidation, in a series of threats against the French that emphasize the suffering of non-combatants. First he instructs the ambassadors: 'tell the pleasant Prince...his soul | Shall stand sore chargèd...for many a thousand widows | Shall this his mock mock out of their dear husbands, | Mock mothers from their sons...' (1.2.281–6). Through Exeter he bids the French king 'in the bowels of the Lord, | Deliver up the crown...take mercy | On the poor souls...the widows' tears, the orphans' cries, | The dead men's blood, the pining maidens' groans...' (2.4.102–7). And finally he directly threatens the citizens of Harfleur with a litany of lurid atrocities explicitly derived from God's rules of siege warfare in Deuteronomy 20 which brings about the town's surrender (3.3.7–43).

Henry also uses intimidation among his own men to enforce discipline by ordering his friend Bardolph to be hanged for unauthorized plundering and at the same time claiming that such rigour is mercy rather than cruelty: 'We would have all such offenders so cut off... none...upbraided or abused in disdainful language. For when lenity and cruelty play for a kingdom, the gentler gamester is the soonest winner' (3.6.108, 111–14). The king follows Machiavelli who also insists that cruelty is merciful: 'Therefore, a prince must not worry about the reproach of cruelty when it is a matter of keeping his subjects united and loyal; for with a very few examples of cruelty he will be more compassionate than those who, out of excessive mercy, permit disorders to continue...'[4] Rather than contrasting this cynicism with biblical morality, Machiavelli substantiates his claims with the example of Moses: 'He who reads the Bible with discernment will see that, before Moses set about making laws and institutions, he had to kill a very great number of men who...were opposed to his plans.'[5] Here he refers to incidents of rebellion, such as worship of the Golden Calf or Korah's revolt, which Moses responded to with mass executions. It is these God-sanctioned actions that validate the Machiavellian maxim that the end justifies the means: 'Reprehensible actions may be justified by their effects . . . when the effect is good . . . it always justifies the action . . . I might adduce in support of what I have just said numberless examples, e.g. Moses, Lycurgus, Solon, and other founders of kingdoms and republics . . .'[6]

One of the most effective means of producing belief is dissimulation: 'The princes who have accomplished great deeds are those who have cared little for keeping their promises and who have known how to manipulate the minds of men by shrewdness . . . it is necessary . . . to be a great hypocrite and a liar . . .' says Machiavelli.[7] Biblical writers seem to approve of many such shifts: Abraham's deception of Pharaoh (Gen. 12: 13–20), Jacob's deception of his father and uncle (Gen. 27: 18–29, 30: 35–40), Joseph's protracted deception of father and brothers (Gen. chs. 42–4), Ehud's assassination of the Moabite king, Eglon (Judg. 3: 15–31), Nathan's entrapment of David into confessing his own guilt (2 Sam. 12: 1–12). Jesus himself tells his disciples that they must proceed with the wariness of serpents (Matt. 10: 16) and hides his divine power (Matt. 16:20). Trickery is a skill that Henry V learns from both his father-figures, Bolingbroke and Falstaff. Henry IV feigns loyalty to the king he deposes and then solicitude for the one he executes, and he triumphs over his enemies in battle not by valour but with the stratagem of dressing many in the king's coats. Falstaff is the father of lies and disguises. Likewise, just as he robs the robbers and confuses his father's spies, Hal deceives the whole kingdom with appearances both of prodigality and holiness.

Dissimulation serves to disorient and confuse those over whom one wishes to gain power, but it also serves as a device to gather intelligence. Moses is commanded to send spies into the promised land to report on enemy strength, Joshua sends spies into Jericho to recruit Rahab to spy for them, David constantly spies on Saul, and his general Joab maintains surveillance in all camps. God spies on his enemies in Babel and Sodom and on his subjects, such as Adam and Eve, Abraham, Jacob, and Job, as he tests their loyalty with temptations and ordeals. Likewise, Henry V spies on his subjects in the Boar's Head tavern, on his captains and foot soldiers on the night before battle, and on his close friends, Cambridge, Scroop, and Grey, at the outset of the French campaign.

According to Machiavelli, to produce the belief required for political rule, it is as important to be sceptical oneself as it is to manipulate the faith of others. Religious deceptions are required because most people are not rational enough to accept the real truths which such deceptions support: 'Nor in fact was there ever a legislator, who in introducing extraordinary laws to a people, did not have recourse to God, for otherwise they would not have been accepted, since many benefits of which a prudent man is aware, are not so evident to reason that he can convince others of them.'[8] Though it is his intelligence system that has discovered the plot against him, Henry construes his rescue as miraculous evidence of God's special protection and parlays that evidence into a morale-raising prediction of future success in battle:

> We doubt not of a fair and lucky war,
> Since God so graciously hath brought to light
> This dangerous treason lurking in our way
> .   .   .   .   .
> Then forth, dear countrymen. Let us deliver
> Our puissance into the hand of God...
> (2.2.181–3, 186–7)

Here he follows Machiavelli's advice about the efficacy of miracles in creating the 'synergistic' alliance between divine and human energies. Wise leaders will try to create miracles and, more importantly, will reinforce faith in earlier miracles to buttress belief in their own miraculous powers.[9] In secret, the Archbishop admits that he no longer believes in miracles: 'It must be so, for miracles are ceased, | And therefore we must needs admit the means | How things are perfected' (1.1.67–9). He nevertheless also construes Hal's conversion as a supernatural transformation: 'a wonder how his Grace should glean it, | Since his addiction was to courses vain' (1.1.54–5). His wonder is the outcome intended by Henry's overall strategy of dissimulation. To frustrate expectation either by feigning weakness or bluffing strength is as strategic in politics as in poker. Mystification and hiding is a rhetorical means of amplifying the power of revelation. God's obscurity in the Bible, his invisibility and remoteness, makes his voice that much louder when it speaks, whether in thunder on Sinai, out of a whirlwind in Job, or at those moments in the New Testament when he drops the disguise of mortal poverty and is suddenly recognized as a divine presence.

Such appearances and removals of disguise are experienced by the citizenry as another species of miracle. When Hal unmasks his own knowledge of the traitors' conspiracy, they admit their sins and condemn themselves to death. When Hal reveals himself after the robbery at Gad's Hill as one of the 'men in buckram', Falstaff manages to cover any trace of wonder, but when finally 'breaking through the foul and ugly mists | Of vapours that did seem to strangle him' (*1 Henry IV*, 1.2.199–200), Henry takes on the mantle of the true king at the coronation, even the fat man responds by getting real religion. Both playful and awesome, these are the kinds of tricks that Hal, like the God of the Bible and his representatives, seems never to tire of playing.

Though it is not easy to distinguish from the satanic lying of such characters as Richard III or Iago, such dissimulation literally brings a king closer to God, according to several early modern ideologues of the divine right of kings. They draw on a doctrine of mystery of state stipulating that royal dissimulation is not only a requirement for rule but in itself a divine and divinity-generating activity. According to King James, God bestowed on kings a divine wisdom that controls what he calls their 'secretest drifts', the deep strategy of state policy. According to Louis Machon, counsellor to Louis XIV, kings possess magical powers by virtue of their access to secrets and occult wisdom withheld from their subjects: 'It is specifically the violence, obscurity and ineffable quality of the gods that must be imitated . . . the coups d'état are princely imitations of all those attributes of divinity that were thought to be either beyond human power (like miracles) or beyond the laws and moral prescriptions that bound men but not God.'[10]

4

In addition to the providential and the political, Shakespeare could find a third perspective in biblical history, one labelled 'psychohistorical'. This represents the causes of events as both public and private—an interplay among large social forces, family dynamics, and the conflicting components of individual personality. Psychohistory applies the approaches of institutional history and psychology to the biographies of political and religious leaders.[11] In the Books of Samuel and Kings, the personal struggles of monarchs are intertwined with the destiny of the nation. These struggles are most fully explored in the stories of David. Providentially, God chose David as the founder of a royal dynasty, the creator of a great empire and forerunner of Messiah. Politically, David acts like an exemplary prince, defending the people against foreign enemies as well as maintaining royal authority despite faction and betrayal. But personally, David is portrayed in the Bible as emotionally vulnerable, morally fallible, and psychologically complex—the lover of Michal and Bathsheba, the betrayer of Uriah, the victim of his beloved son, Absalom. Such traits made him a particularly popular subject of Renaissance art and drama. David Evett delineates three psychohistorical themes in the biblical story of David that shape Shakespeare's second tetralogy: 'first, the relation of public obligations and private desires of rulers; second, the conflicts between the demands of humanity and those of authority; third, the effects on political events of family relationships'.[12] Shakespeare's depiction of the king's dark night of the soul on the eve of the final battle in Act 4, Scene 7 of *Henry V* links Henry's trials with those of David; David's precursor, Moses; and David's descendant, Jesus.

According to the chorus's providential view, the King, in godlike fashion, with 'largess universal, like the sun ... Thawing cold fear' (4.0.43–5) bestows comfort with 'A little touch of Harry in the night' (l. 46) upon the 'ruined band' of the 'poor condemnèd English', who 'Like sacrifices, by their watchful fires | Sit patiently and inly ruminate | The morning's danger' (4.0.22–5). But after his morale-raising banter with the lords, Henry's warmth is shown to be a pretence when he asks Erpingham for his cloak and admits that he needs to be alone for a while in the moonlight before he can continue encouraging the other officers.

The cloak serves him in several ways. First he uses it to disguise himself as a captain, 'Harry Le Roi', to spy on the men in order to determine the strength of their support and to root out weak morale, for he knows that if he appears as himself, his subjects will tell him, like any higher power, only what they think he wants to hear. Eavesdropping on Pistol, Gower, and Fluellen produces evidence of their full support, and so he moves on. The conversation between Court, Bates, and Williams is less reassuring: '[the king] may show what outward courage he will, but I believe as cold a night as 'tis, he could wish

himself in Thames up to the neck. And so I would he were and I by
him, at all adventures, so we were quit here' (4.1.113–16).

So sound those of little faith among the Israelites: 'Oh that we had
died by the hand of the Lord in the land of Egypt, when we ate by the
fleshpots, when we ate bread our bellies full: for ye have brought us out
into this wilderness, to kill this whole company with famine' (Exod. 16:
3). These are the troublesome subjects whose 'lukewarmness', according to Machiavelli, 'partly stems . . . from the scepticism of men, who
do not truly believe in new things unless they have actually had
personal experience of them'.[13] Harry tries to counter their hopeless-
ness with assurances of the king's exemplary valour and their cynicism
with biblical parables and equivocating casuistry justifying the righteousness of the war, but none of these efforts work to produce the kind
of belief he feels he needs.

This is the one time Henry fails, and he is so frustrated that he
almost exposes himself with a threat against Williams (4.1.206). Were
he to do this he might gain Williams's apology but lose the power over
him that secrecy confers. Instead, echoing their complaints—what the
Bible refers to repeatedly as 'murmurings'—he complains to God:

> Upon the King.
> 'Let us our lives, our souls, our debts, our care-full wives,
> Our children, and our sins, lay on the King.'
> We must bear all. O hard condition,
> Twin-born with greatness: subject to the breath
> Of every fool, whose sense no more can feel
> But his own wringing.
>
> (4.1.227–33)

Moses reflects the lukewarmness of the people in his own murmurings:

> Why have I not found favour in thy sight, seeing that thou hast put the charge
> of all this people upon me? Have I conceived all this people? Where should I
> have flesh to give unto all this people? For they weep unto me, saying, 'Give us
> flesh that we may eat.' I am not able to bear all this people alone, for it is too
> heavy for me.   (Num. 11: 11–13)

The frustration arises not so much from the inconsequential political setback, as from the failure of another motive covered by Henry's

cloak: he too needs a little touch of warmth. For, like Moses, Henry experiences his own inner lukewarmness. Upon leaving Erpingham, he had admitted that 'I and my bosom must debate awhile' (4.1.32), and to the soldiers he utters a lengthy description of the king's personal vulnerability: 'I think the King is but a man, as I am ... when he sees reason of fears, as we do, his fears, out of doubt, be of the same relish as ours are. Yet, in reason, no man should possess him with any appearance of fear, lest he, by showing it, should dishearten his army' (ll. 101, 108–12). The disguise here is thinning. Harry Le Roi speaks more frankly than Henry the Fifth ever could, but, ironically, the soldiers react to his plea for their support as if it were only manipulative dissimulation.

As he moves away from the soldiers, Henry uncloaks himself fully. Heard only by the spying audience, in soliloquy he unveils the mystery of state. His royalty, his godlike divine right, is mere dissimulation performed by monarch–actor and applauded by subjects–spectators. His unceremonious encounter with Williams, Court, and Bates has taught him that he is nothing without ceremony, that ceremony itself is at once king and god, and that all are mere idols: 'And what have kings that privates have not too, | Save ceremony, save general ceremony? ... What kind of god art thou, that suffer'st more | Of mortal griefs than do thy worshippers'? (4.1.235–9).

His acknowledgement resembles the tormented recognitions of other Shakespearian military leaders who have lost faith in their own self-projections—Brutus, Lear, Antony, and Coriolanus—and it also alludes to King David in exile, and as speaker of many of the Psalms; to the suffering servant in Isaiah; and in particular to the internal struggle of Christ during his vigil at Gethsemane and on the cross, when he 'cried to God in a loud voice saying "Eli, Eli lama sabacthani?", that is, "My God, my God, why hast thou forsaken me?"' (Matt 27: 46), words quoted from the opening of David's Psalm 22, as noted by the Geneva gloss. This identification is itself another 'mystery of state', what Donaldson calls 'a royal kenosis':

The prince, imitating a divinity who put off his divinity in Christian love in order to achieve the salvation of the world, puts off an ideal and otherworldly goodness in order to achieve the safety of the people, exchanging contemplative perfection for morally flawed action ... the idea that the king is an imitator of God ... includes mimesis ... of those modes of divine action that entail a lowering of the divine nature. . . . It is only a good prince who will hazard his own salvation to seek that of the subjects whom he governs.[14]

Reconceiving his despair and weakness as itself an attribute of divinity, Henry can again dissimulate authority in a brief encounter with Erpingham, who interrupts him for a moment to remind him of his officers' need for the King's presence.

Alone once more, perhaps having returned the cloak to its owner, the King addresses God directly in a mode of discourse even less performative than soliloquy—prayer. We see him encountering the existential reality of God-in-the-trenches rather than projecting the ideological spectacle of 'God for Harry'. And yet what does he seek at this moment of truth? 'Steel my soldiers' hearts. Possess them not with fear' (4.1.286–7). His request is for morale—the very spiritedness that his own public performance is expected to produce, that which the soldiers and the lords ask of him, and he, as Harry Le Roi, has asked of them. His 'God of Battles' is imagined not as one who will bring victory through a miraculous defeat of the enemy, but rather as one who will succeed where Henry has just failed, in buttressing his men's courage and faith. As if to instruct God, he specifies the means by which to achieve this effect: 'Take from them now | The sense of reck'ning, ere th' opposèd numbers | Pluck their hearts from them' (4.1.287–9). It is to blind them from the truth, to cloud their thinking, to reinstitute ceremonial dissimulation.

This request for falsehood slides into another uncomfortable revelation of truth: 'Not today, O Lord, | O not today, think not upon the fault | My father made in compassing the crown' (ll. 289–91). He again begs God to hide the truth, but now from Himself. In other words, Henry prays that God will help him deceive his own conscience, like the King in *Hamlet*, 'a man to double business bound' (3.3.41). But also like Claudius, Henry is again frustrated. Instead of being granted forgiveness, he is further reminded of his guilt and failure:

> I Richard's body have interrèd new,
> And on it have bestowed more contrite tears
>
> .   .   .   .   .
>
> And I have built
> Two chantries . . .
> . . . More will I do,

> Though all that I can do is nothing worth,
> Since that my penitence comes after ill,
> Imploring pardon.
>
> (4.1.292–3, 297–302)

No matter how he tries to cover them, the king cannot escape the knowledge of the secrets he keeps. Sanctimonious action, whether in the form of daily penances of solemn priests or the holy war against France, fails to produce a feeling of innocence. Both God and king must rule by the art of dissimulation and yet never be themselves deceived.

This is the burden of the mystery of state that will keep him forever imploring pardon. But simply setting it down for a moment in private allows him to gather the strength to carry it further. For that burden is also a magic instrument, an occult wisdom that gives him the sense of superiority over all other humans. Now he can respond to his importunate brother Gloucester by saying, 'I will go with thee. | The day, my friends, and all things stay for me' (4.1.304–5).

5

That the institution of kingship itself is constructed as sacred by profane methods and that it inevitably takes a heavy personal toll even from its most successful embodiments are recurrent themes of Shakespeare's second tetralogy of history plays. This ambivalence may partially derive from the Bible's conflicted views of monarchy. God institutes it as a gift of God to the Israelites: 'Tomorrow about this time I will send thee a man . . . him shalt thou anoint to be governor over my people Israel, that he may save my people out of the hands of the Philistines: for I have looked upon my people, and their cry is come unto me' (1 Sam. 9: 16). But in other passages the creation of monarchy appears as a product of the people's betrayal of themselves and their rebellion against God:

> they have cast me away, that I should not reign over them. . . . This shall be the manner of the King that shall reign over you: he will take your sons, and appoint them to his chariots, and to be his horsemen, and . . . to ear his ground, and to reap his harvest, and to make instruments of war. . . . And ye shall cry out at that day, because of your King, whom ye have chosen you, and the Lord will not hear you at that day. (1 Sam. 8: 7, 11–12, 18)

Like all Shakespeare's kings, the individual kings of the Bible are portrayed under double judgement. Saul is a charismatic general who succeeds in securing territory by uniting the tribes against the Philistines, but he arrogates too many powers to himself and is driven insane. He is succeeded by David, God's favourite and beloved by the people. But after displaying the self-abnegating loyalty to his master, the brilliance in battle, and the genius in diplomacy to build a great empire, David too is punished for betraying God and his subjects in a scandalous sexual intrigue. David's son, Solomon, builds on his father's achievements and attains distinction as the wisest of men, turning the empire into a showpiece of wealth and culture, but his glory is eclipsed when his sons once again divide the kingdom and plunge it into civil wars which eventually result in foreign conquest. Likewise, Shakespeare's Epilogue to *Henry V* admits that King Henry, 'This star of England', who, 'the world's best garden . . . achieved' (l. 7), reigned only a 'small time' (l. 5), and his efforts to found a lasting dynasty met failure soon after his death. When the human condition is shown as subject to such a double bind of judgement, the perspectives of history begin to converge with those of tragedy.

'Within a Foot of the Extreme Verge': The Book of Job and King Lear

1

Out in the weather a naked old man howls. Fallen from eminence, betrayed by his loved ones, crazed with illness and grief, he shakes a fist at the sky. To a reader of Shakespeare and of the Bible, he seems familiar. But is it Lear or is it Job? Jan Kott called *King Lear* a 'new Book of Job'.[1] The two works recall one another not only through verbal echoes, thematic parallels, and similarities in plot, but also through their remarkable intensity. To read either is, in the words of John Keats, 'to burn through . . . the fierce dispute | Between damnation and impassioned clay'.[2] Both works attract superlatives. Stephen Mitchell, a recent translator, calls the Book of Job 'the greatest Jewish work of art'.[3] Coleridge called *King Lear* 'the most tremendous effort of Shakespeare the poet',[4] and Harold Bloom commented that 'Like *King Lear*, which is manifestly influenced by it, the Book of Job touches the limits of literature and perhaps transcends them.'[5]

Considering the Book of Job and *King Lear* in tandem allows their parallel elements of plot, character, theme, and language to illuminate one another. Study of these parallels can reveal how Shakespeare's imagination may have been inspired by the Bible and also how he responded to the earlier text with interpretative revision. Such study can also highlight the changes produced by adapting an ancient sacred text into an early-modern theatrical script. Comparing some contrary critical interpretations of each emphasizes the final indeterminacy of meaning in two works that share an equal urgency of ultimate concern.

2

Moses and Henry V are the superlative leaders of their nations. Deuteronomy names Moses the greatest of all prophets (34: 10), and Shakespeare's chorus names Henry V as 'the mirror of all Christian kings' (2.0.6). Concern with leadership belongs to the genre of history. That genre occupies the first half of the Old Testament, which is ordered by chronology and tells the history of the Jews from the beginning of time to their return to Israel following captivity by the Babylonians in the fifth century BCE in a roughly continuous series of books extending from Genesis to Esther.[6] In the second section of the Old Testament, chronological order gives way to grouping by literary convention: a collection of devotional lyrics (the Psalms), a collection of love lyrics (the Song of Solomon), a collection of wise sayings (Proverbs), and a lyrical-philosophical meditation (Ecclesiastes). The first of these non-historical works is a tragic drama: the Book of Job.

Like the Old Testament, the first collection of Shakespeare's plays is organized by genre, as its title indicates: *Mr. William Shakespeare's Comedies, Histories and Tragedies.* After he completed *Henry V,* his ninth history play, in 1599, Shakespeare stopped writing histories for many years. In *King Lear,* as generally in tragedy, emphasis shifts from the local to the universal, from the chronological to the mythic, from what individuals did to what they experienced. Events in *King Lear* take place not among English, but among prehistoric Britons. Similarly Job, the first of the non-historical books of the Bible, is set outside chronology 'in the land of Uz', a vaguely specified place outside the land of Israel. In both works much of the action takes place in a no man's land—a dunghill or a heath.

The idea that the Book of Job is a tragedy was formulated in the fourth century by Theodore of Mopsuestia, and it was supported in the sixteenth century by the Renaissance biblical critic Theodore Beza.[7] The book's emphasis on self-conscious poetic devices—dramatic dialogue, grandiose sound patterns, luxuriant metaphor, irony, and sarcasm—rather than on chronicle, law, or homily, also differentiates it from anything in the historical sections of the Bible. Sir Philip Sidney mentions 'the writer of Job' along with 'David in his Psalms; Solomon in his Song of Songs, in his Ecclesiastes, and his Proverbs; Moses and Deborah in their hymns' as examples of the extraordinary literary value of biblical poetry.[8]

The Book of Job critiques two underlying principles of the preceding historical chronicles: that the Bible should concern itself with God only in relation to his chosen Israelite people, and that God works in history by punishing the wicked and rewarding the righteous. Modern scholars refer to this second principle as the Deuteronomic doctrine because it is so strongly asserted in the last section of the Pentateuch, Deuteronomy, and in the sequence of books following it, referred to as the Deuteronomic History. Job's three friends repeatedly support this doctrine, but Job repudiates it, insisting that much suffering is unmerited and the wicked are often rewarded. After their long debate, God himself finds that Job speaks 'the thing that is right' (42: 7) and thereby seems to revise his own earlier precepts.

The tragedy of *King Lear* similarly questions the orthodox providential outlook of the histories, whose two tetralogies conclude with the triumphs of Henry V and Henry VII, the righteous and God-favoured English leaders. In the *True Chronicle History of King Leir*, Shakespeare's main source for *King Lear*, the providential pattern and the triumph of the King at the end are reinforced by a repeated reference to the biblical God who 'is just and vengeful against sinners . . . instills conscience and remorse for evil and provides "heaven's hate, earth's scorne and paynes of hell" as well as the blessings of immortality'.[9] By contrast the deity in *King Lear*, though desperately called upon in sincere prayer, remains silent while the good are punished along with the evil. This King is not restored to his throne and his state is left tottering.

Along with the biblical books of Ecclesiastes and Proverbs, the Book of Job belongs to 'Wisdom Literature', a category of ancient texts that question God's plan and purpose. Wisdom or 'Sophia' is what Socrates and the other Greeks who called themselves philosophers loved and pursued. Wisdom, or *ḥokmâ* in Hebrew, is both the teacher and the principle by which God created the universe (Prov. 3: 19). Some Wisdom works expressed enlightened optimism—that wisdom is easy to find through instruction: 'For the Lord giveth

wisdom, out of his mouth cometh knowledge and understanding'
(Prov. 2: 6). Others suggested that truth was unknowable because of
the limits of human knowledge: 'But where is wisdom found? And
where is the place of understanding? Man knoweth not the price
thereof: for it is not found in the land of the living' (Job 28: 12–13).
Some, like Ecclesiastes, were even more sceptical: 'For in the multitude of wisdom is much grief: and he that increaseth knowledge,
increaseth sorrow' (1: 18). Such pessimistic wisdom is often expressed
in tragedy: 'Zeus . . . lays it down as law | that we must suffer, suffer into
truth . . . ripeness comes as well.'[10] Like Job, *King Lear* is part of this
Wisdom Literature tradition. Wisdom is what Lear seeks from Poor
Tom, whom he refers to as 'my philosopher' (3.4.165), and a 'good
Athenian' (l. 169).[11] 'Wisdom' is taught by Lear to Gloucester: 'I will
preach to thee. Mark. . . . When we are born, we cry that we are come |
To this great stage of fools' (4.5.176–9), and then reiterated by Edgar:
'Men must endure | Their going hence even as their coming hither. |
Ripeness is all' (5.2.9–11). Tragedy is Wisdom Literature dramatized.

3

Aristotle declared that the 'the soul of tragedy is the plot', which he
defined as 'the imitation of a complete and whole action having . . . a
beginning, and a middle and an end'.[12] Job and *King Lear* share a
similar plot. Both begin with what biblical and Shakespearian critics
call a 'folk-tale motif'—a test of love by which the ruler subjects his
most faithful subjects to a humiliating ordeal to test and prove their
loyalty. Just as God strips his servant Job to impress Satan, Lear strips
his daughter Cordelia in the presence of his court. But before the end
of the first act, Lear himself joins Cordelia and Job as the victim of
incomprehensible punishment.

In the middle part of the story, Job and Lear face poverty, neglect,
and illness that lead them to an encounter with cosmic nothingness
and a loss of self-control. First attracted by quiescence and suicide, and
then resistant, they rage against their fates with curses and lamenta-
tions. They argue bitterly against false comforters—wife, friends, and
daughters—who try to shame, reproach, and frighten them.

At the end of both stories, each protagonist experiences a divine or
quasi-divine encounter with the one whose presence he most longs

for: Job with an angry God who causes him both regret and comfort, Lear with an angelic daughter who is merciful and nurturing. This encounter completes the process of humbling and self-discovery and validates his side in the battle with his opponents. At the end of the Book of Job, after the divine encounter, the protagonist is restored to the privileged position he filled at the outset and dies at a peaceful and prosperous old age. In Lear, after the joyous encounter, the hero is restored to his sanity, his family, and his throne (4.6.70). The Lear plot diverges from Job's in the last scene, when the murder of his daughter plunges the old king back into agony and he dies experiencing an ambiguous final vision. *King Lear*'s secondary plot, tracing the actions of his contemporary, the Earl of Gloucester, has a similar outline. It begins with an old man's fall from grace into an ordeal of disproportionate suffering which leads to a desire for death, a new level of self-knowledge, and an encounter with a kind of divinity. At the end, his lost good child is restored to him and he too dies in a mixture of ecstasy and grief.

Both the Book of Job and *King Lear* contain the ingredients Aristotle attributed to the best tragic plots: reversal of fortunes, or peripety, and discovery, or recognition.[13] In the first two chapters, Job's prosperity is reversed as he tumbles from prestige, wealth, health, and spiritual well-being into isolation, poverty, illness, and spiritual doubt. At first his attitude is patient, but it shifts in the presence of his friends, when after seven days of silent prostration he erupts into a violent curse of the day he was born and a wish for death. After they claim to speak for God, rebuke Job, and advise him to repent for the sin which must have prompted his punishment, he shifts again, affirming his own existence, condemning them, and insistently questioning God for judging him unfairly. The second reversal in the action—one of restoration—occurs when God comes out of hiding, reveals some of the mysteries of his creation, and addresses Job's questions, but only by mocking them. Job repents of what he has said and abandons his grievance. The comforters who claimed to speak for God are rebuked, while Job is vindicated as their redeemer and rewarded with the replacement of his lost goods.

Lear experiences the reversal of misfortune during his self-serving abdication ceremony when his favourite daughter Cordelia is forced to abandon him, and Regan and Goneril conspire to humiliate and expose him. By the middle of the second act he has lost his lands, his retainers, his authority, and his wits. The reversal to restoration occurs in the fourth act when he is rescued by his daughter Cordelia. Reduced to weakness and shame, he expects only punishment but instead is rewarded with love and consideration. Despite the defeat of their armies at the beginning of Act 5, he feels completely fulfilled by the prospect of living out his days in her company. A last-minute reversal to misfortune occurs with the murder of Cordelia, but it is partially mitigated by his own satisfaction in killing her attacker, the destruction of his enemies, and possibly by his dying hope of her recovery in this world or the next.

Recognition, also referred to as agnorisis, or discovery, is the subjective correlative of reversal in the action. It denotes the character's shift of perception, perspective, and attitude that develops as the plot unfolds.[14] As suggested by its etymology, recognition implies that the character discovers a deeper truth that somehow was already known but ignored. Both the Book of Job and *King Lear* trace the way the misfortune of the first reversal strips characters of existing beliefs in benevolent gods, the political and moral order, and the value of life, and causes them to discover disillusioned and sceptical truths. The second reversal brings a new outlook incorporating the lessons of loss.

During Job's first reversal he recognizes that the goods that he had cherished—wealth, family, prestige, friendship, and spiritual complacency—are fragile, a suspicion he harboured even in prosperity. He discovers that those he supported could not be depended upon. He learns that neither pious acceptance nor blasphemous protest will change the course of his fate, that pain can worsen and continue long beyond the point it seems unbearable. He realizes that the righteous and the wicked often do not get what they deserve and that his own unmerited suffering is shared by many others.

Through his second reversal, Job learns that God's action cannot be predicted, comprehended, or limited by human judgements; that nature in both its destructive and creative aspects has a beauty that passes understanding; that counter to what his comforters assert, suffering is not a sign of guilt, and righteousness is worth pursuing even if not rewarded. In his direct encounter, Job finds not only his own insignificance in the face of God's grandeur, but also his capacity to receive, withstand, and feel blessed by God's direct attention: 'I have heard of thee by the hearing of the ear, but now mine eye seeth thee. Therefore I abhor my life, and repent in dust and ashes' (42: 5–6). This capacity is acknowledged when God designates him as a more accurate interpreter of the truth than his antagonists and as a suffering servant, a redeemer whose pain serves to shield them from punishment.

During Lear's first reversal, he discovers a range of follies to which he has succumbed. He learns the imprudence of dividing and giving away his kingdom and expecting nevertheless to retain sovereign power. He also learns the folly of believing flatterers: 'They told me I was everything; 'tis a lie, I am not ague-proof' (4.5.104). Sharing the experience of those on the wrong side of the law, he sees the hypocrisy and incompetence of the justice system that as king he was responsible for. He realizes that the 'heavens', who he thought would make his cause their own, were as merciless as his daughters: 'Here I stand your slave, | A poor, infirm, weak and despised old man' (3.2.19–20). In his debasement, Lear first notices the support of his poor retainers and begins to reciprocate. 'My wits begin to turn. | Come on, my boy . . . Art cold? | I am cold myself . . . Poor fool and knave, I have one part in my heart | That's sorry yet for thee' (3.2.67–73). Their love for him awakens his attention to all those in the kingdom he has previously ignored: 'Poor naked wretches . . . O I have ta'en | Too little care of this' (3.4.28, 32–3). At the fulfilment of the second reversal, when his health, his sanity, and his dignity are restored to him, Lear recognizes his own body—'Let's see: | I feel this pin prick' (4.6.47–8); his own mind—'I am a very foolish, fond old man' (l. 53); and the presence and love of his daughter—'For as I am a man I think this lady | To be my child, Cordelia' (ll. 62–3). Joining her, he awakens to an ultimate reality: 'the mystery of things | As if we were God's spies' (5.3.16–17), which foretells his final unutterable epiphany: 'Look there, look there' (5.3.287).

In addition to reversal and recognition, Aristotle names the third component of the tragic plot 'suffering . . . which results from painful or destructive action such as death on the stage, scenes of very great pain, the infliction of wounds, and the like'.[15] The most disturbing suffering to watch is that inflicted on the weak by the powerful. In the Book of Job and *King Lear*, interrogation, browbeating, and torture are repeatedly endured by those in the grip of higher authorities. God and Satan may be seen to wager playfully as to how their innocent subject will react after God says, 'Lo, he is in thine hand, but save his life' (2: 6). Job is afflicted with boils and nightmares and harangued by three friends who blame the victim and try to make him confess to fabricated crimes. In *King Lear*, Gloucester is tied to a chair and his eyes are gouged out by the Duke of Cornwall who smugly warns, 'Though well we may not pass upon his life | Without the form of justice, yet our power | Shall do a curtsy to our wrath, which men | May blame but not control' (3.7.23–6). Kent is locked in the stocks all night, naked Edgar shivers in the storm, Lear imagines himself bound on a wheel of fire. Kent's concluding lines speak of 'the rack of this tough world' (5.3.290).

Another form of suffering inflicted in the Book of Job and *King Lear* is the continuous stripping down of a formidable personage into someone who has nothing and is nothing. Job's wealth is enumerated at the opening of the book: 'And he had seven sons, and three daughters. His substance also was seven thousand sheep, and three thousand camels, and five hundred yoke of oxen, and five hundred she asses' (1: 2–3). These possessions are taken in quick succession: 'There came a messenger and said: "the Sabeans came violently and took them: yea they have slain the servants... and I only am escaped alone to tell thee." And whiles he was yet speaking, another came... And whiles he was yet speaking, another came...' (1: 14–18). Job tears his robe, shaves his head, and lies down in the dust. 'Naked came I out of my mother's womb and naked shall I return thither' (l: 21), he says. Then he loses his health, his home, and his recognizable appearance. *King Lear* too creates the queasy feeling of the bottom dropping out with images of stripping, invoking the recurrent biblical motif of nakedness as a divestment of kingship. Lear strips Cordelia of her inheritance as he bargains down her value. After relinquishing his lands, he is stripped of his retainers, of the roof over his head, and eventually of the clothes on his back: 'Off, off, you lendings! Come, unbutton here' (3.4.102–3). Edgar experiences a similar reduction as he is stripped of Gloucester's patrimony and reduced to the 'most poorest shape | That ever penury in contempt of man | Brought near to beast' (2.2.170-2), approaching closer and closer to the limiting condition of 'nothing': 'That's something yet. Edgar I nothing am' (2.2.184).[16]

Such material reduction is accompanied by reduction of respect. Both great men are subject to humiliation by inferiors. Job's messengers are sardonic, his wife is scornful, and his friends go from silent sympathy to reprimand—'Behold, blessed is the man whom God correcteth: therefore refuse not thou the chastising of the Almighty' (5: 17)—and then to indictment: 'How long wilt thou talk of these things? And how long shall the words of thy mouth be as a mighty wind?' (8: 2). Lear is first gently and justifiably corrected by Cordelia, then curtly and sarcastically lectured by Goneril, then insulted by her servant, then condescended to by Regan—'O sir, you are old. . . . You should be ruled and led | By some discretion that discerns your state | Better than you yourself' (2.2.319, 321–2).

After being stripped of wealth, power, health, and dignity, all that Job and Lear have left are their beliefs, their confidence that things will get better and eventually make sense. Job has feared, served, and loved God all his life. At first his faith sustains him in affliction: 'The Lord hath given and the Lord hath taken: blessed be the name of the Lord' (1: 21). But as his ordeal continues, he feels abandoned by a master he can no longer trust: 'He destroyeth me with a tempest and woundeth me without cause. He will not suffer me to take my breath, but filleth me with bitterness . . . should God laugh at the punishment of the innocent?' (9: 17, 23). Lear grieves for the familial and ethical bonds he thought held the world together. He tries to invoke the gods that he has assumed protected him both as a king and as an elder: 'O heavens, | If you do love old men . . . if you yourselves are old, | Make it your cause! Send down and take my part' (2.2.362–5). But he finds their neglect as cruel as his children's: 'Here I stand your slave, | A poor, infirm, weak and despised old man' (3.2.19–20).

One thing that is not stripped from either Lear or Job is the power of speech. As their sufferings increase, so does the intensity and eloquence of their language. The language of tragedy, according to Aristotle, 'has been artistically enhanced by . . . linguistic adornment . . . I mean . . . rhythm and harmony and song'.[17] The 'linguistic adornments' in Lear and Job are onomatopoeic representations of painful cries. After seven days and nights of silent build-up, Job explodes:

Let the day perish, wherein I was born, and the night when it was said, 'There is a man child conceived'. Let that day be darkness, let not God regard it from above, neither let the light shine upon it, but let darkness, and the shadow of death stain it: let the cloud remain upon it, and let them make it fearful as a bitter day.   (3: 3–5)

Lear too, though unable to call down universal chaos, absorbs some of the destructive energy that torments him in his verbal expression of agony:

> Blow, winds, and crack your cheeks! Rage, blow,
> You cataracts and hurricanoes, spout
> .   .   .   .   .
> You sulph'rous and thought-executing fires,
> .   .   .   .   .
> and thou all-shaking thunder,
> Strike flat the thick rotundity o' th' world,
> Crack nature's moulds, all germens spill at once
> That makes ingrateful man.
>
> (3.2.1–9)

In addition to the roar of elements, one hears cries of animal pain: 'He hath taken me by the neck and beaten me . . . his archers compass me round about: he cutteth my reins and doth not spare and poureth my gall upon the ground. He hath broken me with one breaking upon another', screams Job (16: 12–13). 'Howl, howl, howl, howl!' (5.3.232), howls Lear like a beast.

The language of the tormentors is as violent as that of the victims. 'Splendid to read, the verbal equivalent of a thermonuclear explosion . . .'[18] God's speech in Job mimics the voice of the whirlwind from which it thunders:

who is this who darkeneth the counsel by words without knowledge? . . . who hath shut up the sea with doors when it issued and came forth as out of the womb? When I made the clouds as a covering thereof, and darkness as the swaddling bands thereof: When I established my commandment upon it and set bars and doors, and said 'Hitherto shalt thou come but no farther' . . .?

(38: 2, 8–11)

Gloucester's son Edmund roars and blasts as he works himself into a malevolent frenzy: 'Why "bastard"? Wherefore "base" . . . Why brand they us | With "base", with "baseness, bastardy—base, base"—' (1.2.6–10). Such cacophony, bordering on gibberish, fits the decorum of tragedy: 'It recalls the original terror, harking back to a world that antedates the conceptions of philosophy, the consolations of the later religions, and whatever constructions the human mind has devised to persuade itself that its universe is secure. It recalls the original un-reason, the terror of the irrational.'[19]

4

In addition to shrieks and curses, the extreme suffering portrayed in tragedy elicits urgent intellectual questioning. Characters search for understanding of a higher order or general principle to explain their pain, and they express what they have found in utterances that delin-eate the themes of the work. According to Aristotle, 'theme' or 'thought' is another essential component of tragedy, expressed not as a claim by the author but 'that which is found in whatever things men say when they prove a point or . . . express a general truth'.[20] A central theme of both the Book of Job and *King Lear* is the nature of the deity, and both represent that nature in various ways.

The first chapter of the Book of Job seems to depict God as any-thing but 'blameless and upright' like his servant Job. He appears cruel and arch and also insecure—a companion to Satan, the adversary of humanity, whom he is trying to impress with boasts about the virtue of his servant Job. At Satan's goading he agrees to a playful wager that allows the adversary to test Job's loyalty with tortures.[21] This God resembles those pagan deities whom Gloucester appealed to as his eyes were being poked out: 'Give me some help!—O, cruel! O you gods!' (3.7.68), and whom he later indicts: 'As flies to wanton boys are we to th' gods; | They kill us for their sport' (4.1.37–8).

The God who speaks directly to Job near the end of the book is less malevolent but no more merciful. He has created and symbolized himself as Leviathan, the sea monster: 'He maketh the depth to boil like a pot . . . He maketh a path to shine after him: one would think the depth as an hoar head . . . He beholdeth all high things: he is a King over all the children of pride' (41: 22–5). He is like the God of nature who reveals himself in Isaiah 45: 7, 'I form the light, and create darkness: I make peace and create evil: I the Lord do all these things.' In *King Lear* this energetic and ruthless deity manifests itself in various ways. Edmund, the 'natural' illegitimate son of Gloucester, prays to it as he invokes the unregulated energies of desire and aggression that he will tap to topple the legitimate order of society: 'Thou, nature, art my goddess' (1.2.1). Lear links it with the refusal of the world to live up to his expectations at the beginning of the play: 'Ingratitude ... More hideous when thou show'st thee in a child | Than the sea-monster—' (1.4.237–9). Later it is the force that he encounters in the 'wrathful skies' (3.2.43) and 'pitiless storm' (3.4.29), 'the dreadful pother' (3.2.50) of 'the great gods' (3.2.49) from whom he demands an accounting: 'Is there any cause in nature that makes these hard-hearts?' (3.6.36).

Other characters expound an orthodox theology of the deity as creator and enforcer of justice—the one who punishes the evil and rewards the good. Adhering to the institutionalized Deuteronomic teachings of the earlier books of the Bible, Job's friends or 'comforters' believe in such a God and assume that Job's suffering shows he has done something to merit it that he refuses to confess and repent of: 'Is not thy wickedness great, and thine iniquities innumerable? For thou hast taken the pledge from thy brother for nought, and spoiled the clothes of the naked' (22: 5–6). Their theology allows them to construe all apparent evil as a greater good, explained by God's hidden but rational plan. But any comfort to be gained by such theology is discredited both by the reader's knowledge of the falsehood of their accusations and by God's own declaration at the end that they have spoken falsely.

Some characters in *King Lear* share this orthodox theology, and, like Job's friends, try to confirm it with their interpretation of causes and effects. Albany, upon hearing that Cornwall has been killed by a servant after gouging out one of Gloucester's eyes, says, 'This shows you are above, | You justicers, that these our nether crimes | So speedily can venge' (4.2.46–8). Albany ignores the reported fact that the servant was killed and the next reported fact that Gloucester's other eye was also taken. Grateful to the 'judgement of the heavens' (5.3.206) for the deaths of Regan and Goneril, he prays to them for Cordelia—'The gods defend her!' (5.3.231)—a moment before her corpse is carried on stage. And when Edmund piously states the Deuteronomic theology at the beginning of the play—'I told him the revenging gods | 'Gainst parricides did all the thunder bend' (2.1.44–5)—he does so only to gull his father.

In addition to encountering deity as cruel, brutal, and inscrutable, characters in both the Book of Job and *King Lear* expound the theme that the gods are kind. Eliphaz generously imagines that the Lord will heal and save those that he has disciplined: 'For he maketh the wound, and bindeth it up: he smiteth, and his hands make whole.... Thou shalt be hid from the scourge of the tongue, and thou shalt not be afraid of destruction when it cometh.... Thou shalt go to thy grave in a full age, as a shock of corn in due season into the barn' (5: 18, 21, 26). In the midst of an elegy lamenting human mortality, Job imagines God hiding him in the grave to shelter him from God's own passing fit of parental fury and then reviving him and treating him like a doting father playing with his child: 'Thou shalt call me, and I shall answer thee: thou lovest the work of thine own hands' (14: 15). In the midst of a plea for pity from his friends, he states his faith that the same God who afflicts him will some day come to his aid: 'For I am sure, that my redeemer liveth, and he shall stand the last on the earth. And though after my skin worms destroy this body, yet shall I see God in my flesh. Whom I myself shall see, and mine eyes shall behold, and no other for me, though my reins are consumed within me' (19: 25–7).

In *King Lear*, the idea of a healer, saviour, and redeemer is embodied in the figures of Cordelia and Edgar, whose compassion and self-sacrifice allude both to the parental and redeemer God imagined by Job, as well as to the suffering servant of the book of Isaiah and the sacrificial Christ of the New Testament. Cordelia prays to 'kind gods' who can 'Cure this great breach in... Th'untuned and jarring senses ... Of this child-changèd father!' (4.6.13–15). Edgar, while dissimulating, nevertheless speaks a kind of truth to his father when he explains 'the clearest gods, who make them honours | Of men's impossibilities, have preserved thee' (4.5.73–4), for that deliverance is provided in Edgar's very presence. Gloucester responds by revising his concept of the deity from demonic to angelic: 'You ever gentle gods, take my breath from me. | Let not my worser spirit tempt me again | To die before you please' (4.5.215–17), and Edgar reinforces his father's new faith with a religious blessing: 'Well pray you, father' (l. 218).

The gods' role in such unlikely passage from 'impossibility' to 'honour' recurs as a theme in both works. 'Blessed is the man God correcteth' (5: 17) asserts Eliphaz, reversing his earlier assertions that those who suffer are punished by God for some infraction. 'He delivereth the poor in his affliction, and openeth their ear in trouble'

(36: 15). Pent up all night in the stocks, Kent avers that 'Nothing almost sees miracles | But misery' (2.2.156–7). France appreciates Cordelia's poverty from the start:

> most rich being poor;
> Most choice, forsaken; and most loved, despised:
>
> .   .   .   .   .
>
> I take up what's cast away.
> Gods, gods! 'Tis strange that from their cold'st neglect
> My love should kindle to inflamed respect.
>
> (1.1.250–5)

Lear learns that 'The art of our necessities is strange, | And can make vile things precious' (3.2.70–1). Gloucester discovers that 'Full oft 'tis seen | Our means secure us, and our mere defects | Prove our commodities' (4.1.19–21).

The pressure of tragedy which makes people seek divinity and invert their values brings other fundamental questions about the human condition to the fore. 'What is man, that thou doest magnify him, and that thou setteth thine heart upon him?' (7: 17) asks Job. 'Is man no more than this?' asks Lear contemplating Edgar masquerading as the Bedlam beggar. 'Consider him well. Thou owest the worm no silk . . . thou art the thing itself' (3.4.96–100). The same answer is offered in both works. 'How much more a man, a worm, even the son of man which is but a worm?' says Bildad in the Book of Job (25: 6). 'I such a fellow saw, | Which made me think a man a worm' (4.1.33–34), says Gloucester in *King Lear*.

The agony of humanity so reduced to its bare essentials leads to the thought and theme of suicide. Job's wife recommends that he 'curse God and die' (2: 10). Soon after piously silencing her, Job curses the day of his birth, moaning 'Or why was I not hid, as an untimely birth, just as infants, which have not seen the light?' (3: 16), and praising the comforts of the grave. Lear says to Edgar, 'Thou wert better in a grave than to answer with thy uncovered body this extremity of the skies' (3.4.95–6). And Gloucester resolves to take the best way out by jumping off a cliff: 'This world I do renounce . . . Shake patiently my great affliction off!' (4.5.35–6). Gloucester uses the word 'patiently' here in a peculiar sense. For him, suicide becomes a kind of acceptance of a hostile fate, giving up a life of resistance against the gods' 'great opposeless wills' (l. 38). Gloucester's son Edgar is convinced that patience is both morally and psychologically necessary, but for him suicide is the opposite of patience, like Hamlet's impulse to 'take arms against a sea of troubles' (*Ham.* 3.61). Instead Edgar tries to teach his father patience by tricking him with a false miracle and repeated counselling: 'Bear free and patient thoughts' (4.5.80); 'Men must endure | Their going hence even as their coming hither' (5.2.9–10). Lear gives him similar advice—'Thou must be patient. We came crying hither' (4.5.174).

With such patience, Job first responds to his afflictions: 'Naked came I out of my mother's womb, and naked shall I return thereafter: the Lord hath given, and the Lord hath taken it: blessed be the name of the Lord' (1: 21). But after seven days of silence, patience gives way to complaint: 'Therefore I will not spare my mouth, but will speak in the trouble of my spirit and muse in the bitterness of my mind . . . And why dost thou not pardon my trespass? And take away mine iniquity?' (7: 11, 21). This shift to impatience can be regarded as a healthy transition from depression to anger, or as a heroic protest that defines the tragic protagonist against the patient piety of the chorus. At the end of the book, Job returns to humble silence after God addresses him directly, but Job's impatience is what elicited God's response and what finally vindicates him. After telling Lear to be patient earlier, Kent says, 'anger hath a privilege' (2.2.70). Impatient righteous anger is part of what gets Lear into trouble in the first place, but it is also what drives him to kill Cordelia's murderer and express the full range of response to the atrocity of the crime—'O, you are men of stones. | Had I your tongues and eyes, I'd use them so | That heaven's vault should crack. She's gone for ever' (5.3.232–4).

The theme of justice, both divine and human, is central to the thought of characters in the Book of Job and *King Lear.* Job stands upon his record as a pillar of justice in his community: 'I put on justice . . . my judgement was as a robe and a crown. . . . I was a father unto the poor' (29: 14, 16). He is outraged by the violation of the law's Deuteronomical principles he feels in his own torments. Lear remembers his role as dispenser of justice in the kingdom: 'When I do stare, see how the subject quakes! | I pardon that man's life' (4.5.108–9). Though he acknowledges his mistakes, he mounts his own bareheaded defence before the 'dreadful summoners' of the storm: 'I am a man | More sinned against than sinning' (3.2.58–9). Cordelia, Edgar, Kent, the Fool, and Cornwall's servants all have endured miscarriages of justice: 'We are not the first | Who with best meaning have incurred the worst' (5.3.3–4).

Their own experiences of being unjustly punished lead Job and Lear like prophets to protest the suffering of innocents and the reward of the wicked everywhere. 'The earth is given into the hand of the wicked; he covereth the faces of the judges thereof' (9: 24), cries Job. 'He that is ready to fall is as a lamp in the opinion of the rich. The tabernacles of robbers do prosper and they are in safety that provoke God, whom God hath enriched with his hand' (12: 5–6). 'Thou hast seen a farmer's dog bark at a beggar? . . . and the creature run from the cur, there thou mightst behold the great image of authority. A dog's obeyed in office' (4.5.150–5), rails Lear.

In both works, the critique of justice is elaborated through inconoclastic scenes in kangaroo courts that undermine the legitimacy of regular court proceedings. Job and Cordelia are first tested in public show trials by an adversarial prosecutor and judge. After the comforters bring Job to court again, accusing him of unnamed violations of the Deuteronomic law, he turns the tables and devotes long speeches to putting them and their God on the stand. Parodying both the forensic metaphors with which Bildad attacks him and the terms of the covenantal relationship between God and humans invoked in other sections of the Bible, Job addresses a jury with arguments that combine pathetic appeal and sarcastic challenge:

If [man] would dispute with [God], he could not answer him. . . . For though I were just, yet could I not answer. . . . for he destroyeth me with a tempest and woundeth me without cause. . . . If I would be perfect, he shall judge me wicked. . . . For he is not a man as I am that I should answer him if we come together to judgement. Neither is there any umpire that might lay his hand upon us both.   (9: 3, 15, 17, 20, 32–3)

In the Quarto text, Lear stages a disorderly mock trial of the daughters who have subjected him to interrogation and judgement (Q 3.6). Mad Tom is judge, the Fool is prosecutor, and a joint stool is one of the defendants. The trial is broken off by allegations of corruption in the court. In the succeeding scene, which takes place inside his castle, Gloucester is tied to a chair to be tried and punished by Regan and Cornwall, who brags that this procedure is no more than a 'form of justice' (3.7.24). In the next act Lear again stages a trial, this time completely in his mind. Here he decides first to pardon all the accused because their accusers are equally guilty—'none does offend, none, I say' (4.5.164)—and then he screams for the blood of his enemies: 'Then kill, kill, kill, kill, kill, kill!' (4.5.183).

In both works, rage against the oppressor is balanced by compassion for the victims. Job grieves,

They cause the naked to lodge without garment, and without covering in the cold. They are wet with the flowers of the mountains, and they embrace the rock for want of covering. They pluck the fatherless from the breast, and take the pledge of the poor. They cause him to go naked without clothing, and take the gleaning from the hungry. (24: 7)

It is likely Shakespeare recalled this passage when he had Lear cry

> Poor naked wretches, wheresoe'er you are,
> That bide the pelting of this pitiless storm,
> How shall your houseless heads and unfed sides,
> Your looped and windowed raggedness, defend you
> From seasons such as these?
>
> (3.4.28–32)

5

Observing linguistic echoes, thematic parallels, and similarities in plot between the Book of Job and *King Lear* highlights significant contrasts between the two works. As in all the other paired texts considered here, Shakespeare's treatment of biblical materials, like that of many of his contemporaries, shifts the emphasis from theocentric to anthropocentric. In the Bible, God is a primary speaker and protagonist. In *King Lear* the deity remains silent. In fact the most potent theological language of Shakespeare's play reverses the biblical hierarchy by making human choices about human beings the determinants of divine behaviour and approval: 'Take physic, pomp, | Expose thyself to feel what wretches feel, | That thou mayst shake the superflux to them | And show the heavens more just' (3.4.33–6). And later, 'Upon such sacrifices, my Cordelia, | The gods themselves throw incense' (5.3.20–1).

Readers of the Book of Job discover a vast gulf separating humans and God. Though Shakespeare's godlike characters—Prospero, Henry V, and the Duke in *Measure for Measure*—imitate God's practice of hiding from, tricking, testing, and saving his subjects, they remain human. In *King Lear* Edgar plays God to Gloucester by creating an experience of death and rebirth in order to forestall his father from the sin of suicide and to strengthen his patience and faith: 'Why I do trifle thus with his despair | Is done to cure it' (4.5.33–4). But Edgar takes on no divine attributes and the miracle is bogus. Cordelia is several times identified with Christ. She is referred to by the gentlemen as one 'Who redeems nature from the general curse | which twain have brought her to' (4.5.202–3), and she echoes Jesus' words in Luke 2: 49—'I must go about my father's business'—when she states 'O dear father, | It is thy business that I go about' (4.3.23–4). But her humanity and mortality are all the more prominent because of the resemblance.

Another contrast between the biblical and the Shakespearian works appears at their endings. Both Renaissance and modern commentators have taken pains to explain how the conclusion of the Book of Job justifies the ways of God to man. The 'Argument' that prefaces the Book of Job in the Geneva Bible states that Job provides 'the example of a singular patience . . . afflicted not only in body but also in mind by temptations of wife and friends . . . [who] came under pretense of consolation but actually to make him despair. . . . He did constantly resist them and came to good success.' God's repudiation of the orthodox comforters and his apparent sanction of Job's rebellion are disposed of by the commentator's scholastic distinction: '[Job] had good cause and handled it badly—good cause was that man could not know God's secret reasonings; bad handling was that he protested against God. . . . [The comforters] had bad cause in that they wanted to bring him to despair, and good handling in that they maintained God's providence and justice.' Similarly, a modern commentator argues that the Book of Job teaches the lesson that God demands and eventually rewards righteousness if it is coupled with patience: 'The beacon of the righteous is not hope of reward but the conviction that, for man, cosmic wisdom is summed up in the duty to fear God and shun evil, whether or not these virtues bear fruit. . . . The case of Job is a stern warning never to infer sin from suffering (the error of the Friends), or the enmity of God toward the sufferer (the error of Job).'[22]

Many critics contrast these restorative endings with the ending of *King Lear*. Dr Johnson found he could not bear it and preferred the version rewritten by Nahum Tate that allowed Lear and Cordelia to survive. Jan Kott observes that the parallels with the Book of Job serve to mark the ending of *King Lear* not as an adaptation but a bitter Beckett-like parody. 'The book of Job is a theatre of the priests. Whereas in . . . Shakespeare . . . the book of Job is performed by clowns . . . the gods do not intervene. They are silent.'[23] The fact that Albany prays, 'The gods defend her!' (5.3.231), just before Lear carries the dead Cordelia on stage and that when he sees them Kent asks, 'Is this the promised end?' (5.3.238), conveys a nihilistic tragic irony rather than a pious theodicy.

And yet Shakespeare might have also entertained a less orthodox reading of the ending of the Book of Job than the Geneva Bible's commentators. Like many modern scholars, he might have dismissed the final prose section as a pious add-on—a kind of Nahum Tate revision—that detracted from the more tragic conclusion of Job's repentance in dust and ashes. Or he might have been thinking of John Calvin's 'description of the Divinity [that] comes at times to resemble a tyrant who arbitrarily and unpredictably saves and damns, just as in Luther He seems at times the enemy. . .'.[24] Or if Shakespeare read the Bible with the imaginative freedom of modern interpreters such as Carl Jung or Jack Miles, he might have found in the happy ending of the Book of Job the story of a primitive god challenged and transformed by one of his own creatures, an ending like *The Tempest*'s, in which the servant Ariel teaches the master Prospero a lesson about humanity.[25]

On the other hand, Shakespeare might have intended the final section of *King Lear* to reflect the more pious reading of the end of the Book of Job. A. C. Bradley suggested that the play's title be changed to 'The Redemption of *King Lear*' to signify that the final lines allow Lear to reach a transcendent revelation of sacrificial love— Cordelia's as well as his own—a love intensified by loss and comparable to that of Christ and the disciples at the crucifixion.[26] And Paul Siegel regards Lear's final cry as the utterance of his departing soul's sighting of Cordelia's on the way to heaven.[27]

Recent critics have tried to sort out these apparently contradictory endings of both the Book of Job and *King Lear* by attributing them to separate originals of the transmitted text. Most biblical scholars believe that the afflicted Job's last speech of repentance for presuming to understand God (42: 1–6) concludes a verse tragedy that has a different textual source from the book's final prose narrative in which God justifies Job and compensates his suffering (42: 7–17).[28] Two distinct early printed versions of *King Lear* also have different endings. In the Quarto, Lear's dying line is 'Break, heart, I prithee break' (Q 5.3.306). In the Folio, this line is reassigned to the onlooker Kent, and a new inconclusive but possibly hopeful utterance is added as Lear's last words: 'Do you see this? Look on her. Look, her lips. | Look there, look there' (5.3.286–7).

According to Kenneth Muir, 'Job was much in his mind while Shakespeare was writing *King Lear*.'[29] If so, more than one version of the story was in his mind. In the Book of Job, clamorous voices shout each other down, each claiming to speak God's word. To end the dispute, the character named God speaks loudest, but his last words are framed by Job's, by a narrator's, and by those of many later commentators. The plurality of surviving texts and of commentaries also removes certainty about which version of his own play was in Shakespeare's mind while he was writing *King Lear*.

Aristotle says that theme or thought in a tragedy is what the characters say, not what the work as a whole or the author says. Readers are driven to search for the wisdom hidden in the Book of Job and in *King Lear* as urgently as the characters within the works seek the truth, in passages of such intensity that they promise a glimpse of the unknowable. It is a paradox of literary language, particularly the language of biblical and Shakespearian tragedy, that its most profound words are least decipherable—perhaps because they come 'within a foot | Of th'extreme verge' (4.5.25–6).

True Lies and False Truths:
Measure for Measure
and the Gospel

I

The title of *Measure for Measure* comes from a prominent gospel saying of Jesus: 'judge not that ye be not judged. For with what judgement ye judge, ye shall be judged: and with what measure ye mete, it shall be measured to you again.'[1] Biblical references pervade this play, which more than any other of Shakespeare's is constructed like a medieval allegory. Characters are named for abstractions. Vincentio, who is addressed only by his title of Duke, means 'conqueror'. His stand-in, Ludowick, signifies 'famous warrior'. Angelo is 'deputy or messenger of God'. Escalus suggests the scales of justice. Isabella means 'consecrated to God' or 'beautiful soul'. Mariana refers to the 'bitterness of suffering' as well as the intercessory mother of God. Lucio recalls Lucifer, the fallen angel of light and mocking father of lies.[2]

Measure for Measure has the design of a biblical parable. It ends with the lesson of forgiveness implied in its title and taught by parables of Jesus, such as that of the unjust servant, in which a foreman is punished for harshly judging his underling for the very fault he has displayed himself (Matt. 18: 22–35). The play's plot line follows that of the parable of the talents (Matt. 25: 14–30) and of the vineyard (Matt. 21: 33–43) in which departing masters test, observe, and return to distribute reproof and forgiveness. Jesus states that in these stories the master stands for God and the servants for humanity. In the oblique style of parabolic discourse, Shakespeare also hints that his Duke represents the Lord. The play's terse opening dialogue— 'Escalus. | My Lord'—recalls God's summons of Abraham: 'Abraham', who answered, 'Here am I' (Gen. 22: 1). When the Duke reveals himself to Isabella at the end of the play, she apologizes like Job: 'O, give me pardon, | That I, your vassal, have employed and pained | Your unknown sovereignty' (5.1.382–4). When Angelo is unmasked and exposed to judgement he says, 'O my dread lord...I perceive your grace, like power divine, | Hath looked upon my passes' (5.1.363, 366–7). Like the gods of *King Lear* and the Book of Job, the God-figures of *Measure for Measure* and the gospels are hidden from the people they tempt, torment, and test. But rather than remaining utterly remote, in these stories they adopt disguises and mingle with those who invoke their names but fail to recognize their presence.

The First Folio places *Measure for Measure* among the comedies, fourth after *The Tempest*. Many critics have labelled it a 'tragicomedy' because of the deepening atmosphere of evil in its first half, but the play has a happy ending in which the blocking law that divides and condemns is abrogated, the errors that created the plot complications are unfolded, and the social order threatened at the beginning appears to be regenerated. 'Measure for Measure' in this sense is a comic formula—like 'tit for tat' or 'quittance'—by which poetic justice is achieved. Other comic conventions used in *Measure for Measure* include secrets and disguises that the audience knows but that characters are blind to, the exposure of a hypocritical puritanical killjoy, and a resolution in which opponents are reconciled, crimes are forgiven, and the drive towards marriage overcomes reluctance from many quarters.

With its happy ending in affirmation of community, redemption of debt, resolution of confusion, overriding of law, and fulfilment of desire, the Christian Bible is also a kind of divine comedy, as suggested by its alternative title of Gospel or 'Good Tidings'. The New Testament is an addition, regarded by Christians as a completion or fulfilment that redirects the pessimistic final movement of the Hebrew Bible towards a happy ending and gives the book as a whole a 'U-shaped' tragicomic plot.[3] Individual gospel narratives share this tragicomic structure. After a downward trajectory towards crucifixion and death, they conclude with resurrection and the return of the departed hero to a triumphant community of new believers. Matthew's gospel also utilizes the comic convention of secret knowledge hidden from most characters but available to the audience, and it creates a gallery of killjoy hypocrites in the Jewish priests and Pharisees. Luke's gospel concludes with a plea for forgiveness for sinners, including those who maligned, conspired against, and betrayed the hero. Revelation, the final book of the New Testament, concludes with the vision of an allegorical marriage.

Measure for Measure also contains elements of a history play. Its opening lines suggest an intention 'Of government the properties to unfold' (1.1.3). It chronicles the effort of Duke Vincentio to strengthen the state against external and internal threats. Like Henry V, he needs to gain control over both enemies and allies in order to achieve his end, but unlike Henry, this 'conqueror' relies upon the means of persuasion and dissimulation rather than warfare and physical punishment. The gospels also are a kind of history. Like the five books of the Pentateuch, which narrate the origins and growth of God's first chosen people and their state, the five opening books of the New Testament chronicle the formation and early development of the new chosen people and their 'kingdom of heaven'. 'We use this name (Gospel) for the histories, which the four Evangelists write', states the Introduction to the Geneva Bible's New Testament. On its title-page appear the same engraving and motto as are on that of the Old Testament: '"The Lord shall fight for you: therefore hold you your peace", Exod.14, vers.14.' At the beginning of the gospels, Jesus is born into the genealogy of David, king of the Jews. And though his kingship is denied by the Jews, at the end it is accepted by a new community recruited from the whole of the Roman empire: 'All power is given unto me in heaven and in earth. Go therefore and teach all nations baptizing them in the name of the Father and the Son and the Holy Ghost' (Matt. 28: 18–19).

Such resemblances of plot, character, theme, and genre between the Bible and *Measure for Measure* have been questioned as often as they have been noted.[4] Many critics acknowledge a significant link between Vincentio and the God of the New Testament, but they disagree as to whether Shakespeare intended to portray him as a benign embodiment of divine power, a malicious abuser of it, or a mere mortal who aspires to be God and fails.[5] Disagreement like this seems appropriate to a play associated with the gospels, for these biblical books are also works of controversy, embattled and battling texts in which the events narrated, the interpretation of those events, and the interpretation of earlier texts remain in contention. Consistent with scriptural references and parallels in his other plays, Shakespeare's work allows for both sides in these debates to be true, like the Bible itself providing a basis for the wide range of readings found by his contemporaries— readings pious, sceptical, and profane. Though tracking the sustained match between Vincentio and the New Testament God may not make the Duke more appealing to those who find him incompetent or immoral, it does make sense out of a play that is often regarded as severely flawed.

2

Identifying himself with God through a paraphrase of Jesus (Matt. 5: 14–16), the Duke selects Angelo to shine forth in virtue: 'Heaven doth with us as we with torches do' (1.1.33). He makes him the dispenser of 'mortality and mercy' in Vienna and hastily departs. The Duke's secret purpose, revealed to the audience in the third scene, is 'to strike and gall' the unruly citizens by appointing a harsh deputy to enforce the laws that he himself has allowed to 'let slip', and at the same time to test the Deputy's integrity once he has been given the Duke's authority, in order to 'see | If power change purpose, what our seemers be' (1.3.53–4). Friar Thomas—named after the doubting disciple (John 20: 25)—is extremely dubious about this project, as have been many critics, for it seems politically impractical as well as ethically compromised. Nevertheless, the Duke's plan resembles the strategy of God the ruler trying to govern recalcitrant humanity with prophets, judges, and kings while at the same time testing his chosen deputies.

That plan is expounded early in the Hebrew Bible and even more clearly in Paul's retelling of Old Testament history in his epistle to the Romans. He says that 'God gave [the people] up to their heart's lusts, unto uncleanness, to defile their own bodies between themselves' (Rom. 1: 24). 'Because that when that they knew God, they glorified him not as God, neither were thankful, but became vain in their imaginations' (1: 21). 'Men though they knew the Law of God, how that they which commit such things are worthy of death, yet not only do the same, but also favour them that do them' (1: 31). The second scene of the play pictures this situation. Lucio and his friends flaunt their disobedience:

LUCIO Thou concludest like the sanctimonious pirate, that went to sea with the Ten Commandments, but scraped one out of the table.

SECOND GENTLEMAN 'Thou shalt not steal'?

LUCIO Ay, that he razed.

(1.2.7–11)

They take pleasure from knowing the law and mocking it. The Duke appoints his deputy Angelo to control them.

In the Bible, after repeatedly failing to discipline unruly humanity with expulsions, curses, floods, and linguistic confusion, God appointed Abraham and his descendants, the Jews, to serve as his chosen deputies. They were to be the bearers and enforcers of the Law he gave to Moses—a nation of priests, the righteous among the Gentiles (Exod. 19: 6). Angelo attempts to cast his light and carry out this role by issuing a proclamation razing the brothels and imposing capital punishment for sexual infractions. That proclamation is modelled on the Old Testament law advocated by Puritan divines who expressed the wish that Moses' death penalty would be restored for punishment of lechery.[6] But, according to Paul, God's initial strategy failed. The law cannot be effectively or fairly applied by God's deputies: 'for by the Law cometh the knowledge of sin' (Rom. 3: 20).

An analogous failure is demonstrated in the response of the Viennese revellers. The deputy's crackdown creates not compliance but reactions of contempt, hostility, and fear towards the law. Lucio calls for an appeal to the Duke, Mistress Overdone frets for her lost business, and Claudio sees the judgement upon him as tyrannical and harsh: 'The bonds of heaven. On whom it will, it will; | On whom it will not, so; yet still 'tis just' (1.2.114–15). Here he alludes to Romans 9: 18: 'he hath mercy on whom he will and whom he will he hardeneth'. Glossing such predestinarian sayings about God's own part in the transgression of sinners, the Geneva Bible states, '. . . the only will and purpose of God is the chief cause of election and reprobation'.[7]

After a comic interlude displaying the failure of the justice system in Vienna, Act 2, Scene 2 reveals the corruption of magistrates by the dual evils of legalism and hypocrisy. Rather than adhering to the spirit of the law to administer equity as Escalus recommends, Angelo sticks to the letter and rejects Isabella's plea that mercy be extended to her brother. The law's power of condemnation kindles his desire for more power, and he demands that she yield to him and commit the very sin for which she pleads forgiveness. Angelo fails the same test that God imposes on his chosen people. They prefer the niceties of ritual over the spirit of righteousness, and their kings, such as Saul, David, Solomon, and Ahab, repeatedly abuse power in pursuit of women and wealth. Echoing the condemnations of such Old Testament prophets as Isaiah, Paul excoriates the Jews for this failure: 'Thou that say'st, a man should not commit adultery, dost thou commit adultery? . . . thou that gloriest in the Law, through breaking the Law dishonourest thou God?' (Rom. 2: 22–3). These Old Testament Jews are the forerunners of the Pharisees whom Jesus accuses of the same sin: 'for outward ye appear righteous unto men, but within ye are full of hypocrisy and iniquity' (Matt. 23: 28).

Isabella's request for mercy seems to counter Angelo's legalism. But at this point in the play, she is no less bound by the law than he is. Even though she cites principles stated by Jesus and Paul, her arguments for forgiveness are just as corrupt as Angelo's for justice. She begins by admitting that what her brother did 'is a vice that most I do abhor, | And most desire should meet the blow of justice' (2.2.29–30) and that she comes to engage in special pleading. It is only with the indecent promptings of Lucio—'You are too cold. . . . Ay touch him; there's the vein. . . . to him, wench! He will relent. | He's coming; I perceive't' (2.2.58, 72, 127–8)—that she warms to the task. Her appeal to the true Christian principle of redemption is tainted by her unconsciously seductive language: 'Go to your bosom; | Knock there, and ask your heart what it doth know | That's like my brother's fault. . . . Hark how I'll bribe you' (ll. 140–2, 149). This seductiveness induces the Deputy to consider a pardon, but also for a wrongful purpose: as exchange for her relinquishing the 'sweet uncleanness' of her body (2.4.53). No less than the sanctimonious pirate, both Angelo and Isabella are bound by what Northrop Frye calls the 'humours of different kinds of legalism'. In order for them to be freed, 'the law must not be annulled or contradicted but transcended; not broken but fulfilled by being internalized'.[8]

In contrast to this convoluted incident of deepening corruption, the next scene displays the beginnings of a straightforward solution to the failures of the law—the preliminary movement of 'gospel' or good news. In spite of his love for 'the life removed' (1.3.8), the departed Duke returns to Vienna to observe and also to aid his fallen subjects, disguised as a humble friar. Having confirmed that his first deputy is unable to carry out his mission, the Duke creates a replacement, initiating an ongoing strategy of double substitution. The second substitute will be reliable because it is actually he himself in disguise. This premiss may seem far-fetched, but it makes good theatrical sense by creating an elaborate plot complication which deepens spectators' suspense. It also parallels the strategy of the New Testament God, who takes on the disguise of a human in order to observe, judge, and substitute for his first failing replacement—the Jews.[9] Paul explains the gospel story of the incarnation of Jesus as just such a disguise: 'Who being in the form of God . . . made himself of no reputation, and took on him the form of a servant, and was made like unto men, and was found in shape as a man' (Phil. 2: 6–7).

'Bound by my charity and my blessed order, | I come to visit the afflicted spirits | Here in the prison. . . . that I may minister | To them' (2.3.3–8) announces the Friar, echoing the account of 1 Peter 3: 19—'he also went, and preached unto the spirits that were in prison'. His first encounter is with Juliet, Claudio's fiancée. He determines that unlike any of his other subjects she has a true allegiance to the law, for she admits her culpability, takes 'the shame with joy' (2.3.37), and welcomes punishment as her due. Recognizing that she has herself made satisfaction, he absolves her, as Jesus healed 'the poor in spirit' (Matt. 5: 3), who made no pretence of righteousness (Matt. 8: 2–8). Were all those the Friar or Jesus encounters to react similarly, there would be no more drama of salvation.

In the next scene, however, the plot thickens and curdles. Angelo's confession of his own sin of lust leads not to repentance but self-division:

> heaven hath my empty words,
>
> .   .   .   .
>
>   God in my mouth,
> As if I did but only chew his name,
> And in my heart the strong and swelling evil
> Of my conception.
>
>   (2.4.2, 4–7)

The conflict is specifically focused on sexual desire: 'Blood, thou art blood. . . . dispossessing all my other parts | Of necessary fitness?' (2.4.15, 22–3). His writhing soliloquy echoes Paul's entrapped humanity: 'what I would, that do I not, but what I hate that do I' (Rom. 7: 15). 'I delight in the law of God concerning the inner man, but I see another law in my members . . . leading me captive . . . to the law of sin' (7: 22–3).

Angelo follows the law of sin in his equivocating proposition to Isabella, urging her to submit to him for the same false reasons she had brought forward in defence of her brother. Caught in a similar Pauline contradiction—'At war 'twixt will and will not' (2.2.33)—she is forced to admit that her earlier pleadings were inconsistent with her own principles and asks for his pardon. His response distils the play's biblical concern with the way expression clouds the distinction between sincerity and hypocrisy: 'We are all frail' (2.4.122). Admitting his own sinfulness and yet hiding it from her, these words lead him not to forgiveness but exploitation: 'Be that you are; | That is, a woman. . . . show it now, | By putting on the destined livery' (2.4.134–8).

When she finally understands his drift, she resorts to the legalistic but also criminal tactic of blackmail, threatening to indict him for criminal extortion unless he agrees to 'Sign me a present pardon for my brother' (2.4.152). He counters this threat with an even more pharisaic response: his official position guarantees that she will not be believed, and unless she yields he will have her brother tortured to death (2.4.154–9).

The return of the Friar in the next scene again produces a contrasting atmosphere of teaching, healing, and forgiveness. He comforts the despairing Claudio by convincing him that the death sentence he is under is no real threat since the life that it would take is no real life:

> Reason thus with life.
> If I do lose thee, I do lose a thing
> That none but fools would keep.
>
> .   .   .   .   .
>
> What's in this
> That bears the name of life?
> (3.1.6–7, 38–9)

In the chapter following the description of the law as the agency of sin and death, Paul similarly argues that 'For they that are after the flesh, favour the things of the flesh. . . . For the wisdom of the flesh is death' (Rom. 8: 5–6). Repudiating life, says the Friar, liberates the spirit: 'Be absolute for death. Either death or life | Shall thereby be the sweeter' (3.1.5–6). At the end of his long speech Claudio agrees: 'I humbly thank you. | To sue to live, I find I seek to die, | And seeking death, find life. Let it come on' (3.1.41–3), echoing Jesus' advice to the disciples: 'He that will save his life, shall lose it, and he that loseth his life for my sake, shall save it' (Matt. 10: 39).

Claudio does not retain his newfound comfort outside his teacher's presence. The Friar leaves to eavesdrop, and Isabella enters the cell to tell Claudio of Angelo's 'loathsome ransom'. When he hears there is a chance his life can be spared, Claudio backslides into subjection to the law of death and sin, fleeing the former and embracing the latter:

> Death is a fearful thing.
>
> .   .   .   .   .
>
> Sweet sister, let me live.
> What sin you do to save a brother's life,
> Nature dispenses with the deed so far
> That it becomes a virtue.
>
> (3.1.116, 134–7)

Like Isabella's to Angelo, his pleas for mercy here are false, because they are based on fear rather than faith. Under pressure of the same law, Isabella reacts in kind: 'Die, perish! Might but my bending down | Reprieve thee from thy fate, it should proceed. | I'll pray a thousand prayers for thy death, | No word to save thee' (ll. 145–8). She is guilty not because of her choice to preserve her chastity and refuse the cruel bargain, but because of her righteous malice that now, like Angelo's, would condemn her brother to death.

3

This is the low point of the story, at which three souls have succumbed to their particular weaknesses and fallen into corruption. The letter of the law without the spirit of compliance has created an impasse in which magistrate rules as criminal, the plea for mercy becomes wheedling temptation, the love of life collapses into dread of death, and the tie of siblinghood turns into exploitation and recrimination. To some critics, these negative outcomes cast doubt upon Vincentio's identification with God. Louise Schleiner states the Duke's 'test results are so discouraging [that] all assertions of divine authority are undermined'.[10] Anne Barton sees their falls as instances of the 'error and miscalculation . . . rife in [Vincentio's] plot'.[11] But in the Bible, such temporary failures of God to achieve his purpose—whether as Jehovah or Jesus—occur repeatedly, from the fall of Adam and Eve, to the backslidings of the children of Israel and their kings, to the betrayals of Judas and the other disciples. There they are attributed not to God's incompetence but to humanity's frailty, disobedience, or treachery. Barton observes that 'reality is more unpredictable and insubordinate than the Duke suspects; his efforts at scripting are frustrated and he responds with arrangements and patchings'.[12] As additional evidence, she presents the later interlude with Barnardine, a condemned prisoner who obdurately refuses to comply with the Duke's plan to offer him as a ransom for Claudio. However, the failure of this scheme makes the Duke more rather than less Godlike. Barnardine recalls Barabbas the murderer, whom the Jews refuse to accept as a ransom for Jesus, and also Peter, who sleeps through his master's hour of need. 'Unfit to live or die. O gravel heart!', says the Duke as the prisoner rustles in his straw refusing to be awakened (4.3.61). 'Sleep henceforth and take your rest', says Jesus to his snoring disciples, and the Geneva gloss remarks on his sarcasm: 'He speaketh in a contrary sense, meaning they should anon be well wakened' (Matt. 26: 45).

The very analogy that Schleiner uses to discredit the Duke's improvisations brings him further into line with his biblical model: the failures of his earlier schemes 'force him to imitate the legal astuteness of the Pauline God who "found out a remedy" with a kind of divine lawyer's trick'.[13] Orthodox commentators such as Wilson Knight, Battenhouse, and Sarah Velz link this dramatic moment, when the disguised Duke takes direct control over the action, to the moment when God, the ruler who has entered human history disguised as a man, takes upon himself the project of human salvation by fulfilling the demands of the law himself. As Claudio renews his wretched pleading, he is interrupted by the Friar coming out of hiding. Having heard of Angelo's fall and witnessed both Isabella's and Claudio's, the

Friar shifts roles from observer, teacher, and healer to active participant in the 'government' of his subjects.

The Friar first rescues Claudio with a half-truth. He takes him aside and says that Angelo's offer to Isabella to spare him in return for sex was only a test of her chastity and that the death penalty is unavoidable. This restores Claudio to the confidence of his recent conversion—'I am so out of love with life that I will sue to be rid of it' (3.1.173–4)—and enables him to be reconciled with his sister before he departs. Next the Friar turns to Isabel to embark on a more elaborate scheme which he promises will solve many problems at once: 'To the love I have in doing good, a remedy presents itself. . . . You may most uprighteously do a poor wronged lady a merited benefit, redeem your brother from the angry law, do no stain to your own gracious person, and much please the absent Duke' (ll. 200–5).

The word 'remedy' resonates with Isabella's invocation of the gospel story of Christ's atonement on the cross for the sins of humanity, in her earlier appeal to Angelo: 'Why, all the souls that were were forfeit once, | And He that might the vantage best have took | Found out the remedy' (2.2.75–7). The Friar's allusion to this remedy recalls Paul's enthusiastic reversal from the despair of the law of sin and death to the 'good news' of justification by faith: 'It is God that justifieth, who shall condemn? . . . we are counted as sheep for the slaughter. Nevertheless, in all these things we are more than conquerers through him that loved us' (Rom. 8: 33, 36–7). The individual who accepts God's love and control, according to Paul, 'will cry "Abba, Father"' and will recognize that 'the same spirit beareth witness with our Spirit, that we are the children of God' (8: 15–17). Accepting the Friar's invitation, Isabella replies, 'I have spirit to do anything that appears not foul in the truth of my spirit. . . . Show me how, good father' (3.1.207–9, 240).

The Friar's remedy turns out to be a bed trick. Angelo's former fiancée, Mariana, is to sleep with Angelo disguised as Isabella. This plan creates a wrenching shift of register from theological tragedy to fabliau. But the dirty story is a clean version of the 'foul redemption' that the 'man whose blood | Is very snow-broth' (1.4.57) demanded from Isabella as ransom for Claudio's body, and it produces an apt payback for Angelo as well as for Isabella. Participating in this sexual game without actually losing her virginity is 'measure for measure' exchange for her legalistic obsession with chastity. The body substitution at the heart of the bed trick constitutes a comic version of the ransom story of atonement at the centre of gospel theology: 'Even as the Son of man came . . . to give his life for the ransom of many' (Matt. 20: 28).[14] Though this typological connection between bed trick and divine ransom may seem remote, it was familiar to a Renaissance audience exposed to texts that likened the prostitute Mary Magdalen to the dying Christ and to biblical stories of Tamar using a bed trick to conceive Judah's child, Laban using a bed trick to keep Jacob as his farmhand, and the Holy Spirit surreptitiously taking the place of Mary's husband to bring about the Incarnation.[15]

After a survey of the corruption in the prison and a taste of Lucio's slander of legitimate authority—the obverse of Angelo's hypocrisy— the Friar summarizes the condition of humanity: 'there is so great a fever on goodness that the dissolution of it must cure it. . . . This news is old enough, yet it is every day's news' (3.1.480–8). In a speech composed of epigrammatic couplets he explains the 'cure', which requires a twofold 'dissolution' of goodness. He will dissolve the surrogate authority conferred upon his deputy by taking back 'the sword of heaven' (l. 517), and he will restore order himself with means as 'dissolute' as his subjects: 'To draw with idle spiders' strings | Most ponderous and substantial things? | Craft against vice I must apply' (ll. 531–3). Following the formula of comic justice, he will trick the trick- ster: 'So disguise shall, by th' disguisèd, | Pay with falsehood false exacting . . .' (ll. 536–7). His own use of the legalism and deception he has condemned in his subjects is a means justified by the outcome: 'the doubleness of the benefit defends the deceit from reproof' (3.1.259–60); the deception is to be 'a physic | That's bitter to sweet end' (4.6.7–8).

Dissolving goodness to restore it or employing craft against vice also figures prominently in the gospel story. Paul says, 'we approve [prove] ourselves as the ministers of God . . . by honour and dishonour . . . as deceivers and yet true' (2 Cor. 6: 4, 8).[16] Jesus says to his disciples: 'Behold, I send you as sheep in the midst of wolves: be ye therefore wise as serpents, and innocent as doves' (Matt. 10: 16). Near the midpoint of Matthew's gospel he tries to explain to his disciples why he speaks to the people in riddling parables: 'because they seeing, do not see: and hearing they hear not, neither understand. For this people's heart is waxed fat, and their ears are dull of hearing, and with their eyes they have winked' (13: 13–15). In the same position as the prophet Isaiah whom he here quotes, he knows that those who need his teaching most are least capable of accepting it. Therefore, he must proceed by secrecy, indirection, and dissimulation, confounding his allies as well as his enemies.

To enlist co-operation, the Friar partially discloses his true identity to the Provost. He shows a letter with the Duke's hand and seal, announces the Duke's impending return, and allays the Provost's doubts: 'Put not yourself into amazement how these things should be. All difficulties are but easy when they are known' (4.2.203–5). These assurances echo God's preliminary disclosures of his identity with Jesus: 'a voice out of the cloud, saying, "This is my beloved Son, in whom I am well pleased: hear him." When the disciples heard that, they fell on their faces and were sore afraid. Then Jesus came and touched them, and said, "Arise, and be not afraid"' (Matt. 17: 5–7).

Yet the Friar continues to deceive Isabella. To her anxious query about her brother, he replies, 'His head is off, and sent to Angelo' (4.3.113), disappointing her with the failure of his promise and teasing the audience who have just seen the dead Ragozine's head offered as a substitute. Anne Barton faults the Duke for devising 'special tests' to satisfy 'a scientific curiosity as to how [she and others] will behave under stress'.[17] But the God of the Bible makes a habit of using such tricks to test and strengthen the faith of his own loyal followers such as Abraham, Joseph, Moses, and Job. Jesus can be read as tricking as well as delivering his disciples while they are out in a boat during a storm. He frightens them by walking across the water, and before rescuing Peter, lets him nearly drown (Matt. 14: 24–34). Not until the end of the play will it become clear that another reason the Friar lies to Isabella is to wean her from the pharisaical righteousness that converts frustration and grief into a desire for revenge. Earlier she directed that desire against her brother, whose death she ardently wished for. The Friar's lie allows her to experience the pain of satisfying that wish. Yet it also tempts her once again to channel frustration into a violent desire for vengeance against Angelo. To Ludowick's counsel, 'Show your wisdom, daughter, in your close patience. . . . give your cause to heaven' (4.3.115, 121), she responds, 'O, I will to him and pluck out his eyes!' (4.3.116). This desire must fully surface before it can be purged.

In the next series of apparently random incidents, the Duke-Friar increases his control over everyone, just as God takes greater control of the action when Jesus approaches Jerusalem. From Lucio, he elicits more actionable slander and an unwitting confession to impregnating Kate Keepdown (4.3.166). Like Jesus mystifying the priests and setting them to argue amongst themselves (Matt. 21: 23–5), he confounds Escalus and Angelo with letters announcing the Duke's return. In Act 4, Scene 5 the Duke himself makes a low-key appearance to direct Friar Peter, a substitute for his substitute Friar Ludowick, who of course cannot be there when the Duke himself is present. A similar third-level substitution is carried out in Matthew's gospel shortly before Jesus enters the city. 'And I say also unto thee, that thou art Peter, and upon this rock I will build my Church.... And I will give unto thee the keys of the kingdom of heaven, and whatsoever thou shalt bind upon earth, shall be bound in heaven: and whatsoever thou shalt loose on earth, shall be loosed in Heaven' (Matt. 16: 18–19). It is immediately followed by the charge 'that they should tell no man that he was Jesus the Christ' (16: 20). Just as Jesus' disciples express confusion about what is to come as they are sent on various errands, Mariana and Isabella express fright and puzzlement before Friar Peter gives them their entrance cues and places to stand.

These scenes stake out the different perspectives from which different actors and the audience will observe the play's denouement. Along with Angelo, Mariana, and Isabella, the audience is privy to the secret of the deputy's guilt, which is hidden from everyone else but the Duke and his assistants. Along with Mariana and Isabella, the audience is privy to the secret of the Friar's bed trick and his plan to expose the deputy, hidden from Angelo and everyone else. Along with the Duke, whom the audience alone has just seen on stage, it is privy to the secret that he is the Friar, which is hidden from Mariana, Isabella, and everyone else. But neither the audience nor anyone on stage is yet privy to the secret of why the Friar keeps Isabella in the dark about Claudio's death and what his veiled 'full purpose' is in requiring her to lie to the Duke (4.6.1–8). This elaborate arrangement of sight-lines and obstacles highlights the Duke's omniscience. Though others remain in varying degrees of darkness, nothing is hidden from him. The contrast between his knowledge and their ignorance consolidates his control over his formerly unmanageable allies and enemies, concluding a progressive revelation of his omnipotence from beginning to end of the play.

A similar effect is generated by the development of multiple perspectives in the Bible: those of the crowd of Jews, of the Pharisees and
scribes, of the Roman officials, of the disciples, of the reader, and of
Jesus, who, though he seems to know a great deal, sometimes does not
understand what God has in mind. At its very centre, Matthew's
gospel considers the split between those who are in on the secrets of
the text and those who are not. 'Because it is given unto you to know
the secrets of the kingdom of heaven, but to them it is not given. For
whosoever hath, to him shall be given, and he shall have abundance:
but whosoever hath not, from him shall be taken away, even that he
hath' (Matt. 13: 10–12). According to the Renaissance Platonist Pico
della Mirandola, 'Jesus . . . proclaimed [the Gospel] to the crowds in
parables; and separately to the few disciples who were permitted to
understand the mysteries of the kingdom of heaven, openly and without figures. He did not even reveal everything to those few, since they
were not fit for everything, and there were many things which they
could not endure until the coming of the Spirit taught them all
truth'.[18]

4

The complex and often confusing grand finale which follows these
preparations in *Measure for Measure* is arranged as an expanding set of
climactic conflicts and revelations that parallel the gospel's equally
complex final story of Jesus' entry into Jerusalem, his confrontations
with Pharisees and Romans in large public trials, his mistaken identity,
his humiliation, and his final self-disclosure and triumph. In both
narratives, what appears to be a net closing around the heroes will turn
out to be a net closing around their antagonists.

The fifth act begins with the Duke's grand entrance to the city,
paralleling Jesus' entrance to Jerusalem. Vincentio's greeting to Angelo is interrupted by Isabella's sudden demand for 'Justice, justice,
justice, justice!' (5.1.25). She calls the Deputy 'a murderer . . . an adul-
terous thief, | An hypocrite, a virgin-violator' (ll. 39–41). Although she
and the crowd believe she challenges the Duke, he and we understand
that she has been indirectly coached by him via Friar Peter. The Duke
seems to defend Angelo from these accusations, toying with him and
seeking like Polonius, 'by indirections [to] find directions out' (*Ham.*

2.1.63), pressuring him either to come clean or to condemn himself further. This form of entrapping interrogation is a favourite of the Bible's God. He uses it on his sinful deputies: Adam and Eve and Cain (Gen. 2: 9–11, 4: 9), Joseph's brothers (Gen. 42: 7–38), and David (2 Sam. 12: 1–7). In Matthew, God arranges for Jesus to mount an attack similar to Isabella's just after coming to the city. In the presence of large crowds he goes into the temple, upsets the tables of the money-changers, and drives out those who are buying and selling (21: 12–13). As Isabella is questioned by Angelo and Escalus, Jesus is asked by the chief priests and elders, 'By what authority dost thou these things? And who gave thee this authority?' (21: 21). As Isabella sets Angelo, Escalus, and the Duke arguing, he 'set them arguing amongst themselves' (21: 25), and as Isabella tells the story of Angelo's crimes, Jesus tells three accusatory and threatening parables directed against the Pharisees (21: 28–45).

In addition to working on Angelo, Isabella's staged testimony carries out the Duke's intentions for her. Its half-true claim that Angelo is a 'virgin-violator' allows her to get back at him publicly for his insult to her honour in proposing the foul ransom, but it also forces her to bear the humiliation of appearing in public as a non-virgin and only secretly retaining her sexual purity. This is a lesson to her about the difference between apparent and real holiness which requires her to gain a real rather than a masqueraded sympathy for her brother and Juliet. It also forces her to retreat from her earlier self-righteous insistence that 'More than our brother is our chastity' (2.4.185).

On her way out, Isabella discloses that her collaborator in this indictment of Angelo is Friar Ludowick. The Duke orders Ludowick apprehended, feigning belief in his antagonists' lies. After Angelo once again is placed in the seat of judgement, mystification is intensified by Friar Peter's return with a veiled woman—the first of three hooded figures he will bring on stage—whose riddling discourse confirms that Isabella was lying. When Angelo commands that she lift her veil, he discovers the bed trick. Rather than Isabella, it was Mariana, his lawfully contracted fiancée, who has slept with him. This second public humiliation and indictment temporarily silences him, just as the joined forces of the Pharisees and Sadducees are silenced by Jesus' accusations: 'And none could answer him a word, neither did any from that day forth ask him any more questions' (Matt. 22: 46).

The Duke again departs, stirring up further mischief. Asserting that the Duke is 'in' him, Escalus now takes over the interrogation and threatens to torture Isabella: 'I will go darkly to work with her' (5.1.276). In the gospel story, God abandons his true deputy and disciples to the rage of his false ones. After verbal duels with his opponents, Jesus warns his followers, 'Then shall they deliver you up to be afflicted, and shall kill you, and ye shall be hated of all nations for my name's sake' (Matt. 24: 9). The object of the interrogation is to capture their leader: 'Then assembled together the chief Priests and the Scribes, and the Elders of the people into the hall of the high Priest, called Caiaphas, and consulted how they might take Jesus by subtlety, and kill him' (26: 3–4).

Friar Ludowick is roughly brought before Escalus for questioning: 'Come, sir, did you set these women on to slander Lord Angelo?' (5.1.285–6). To the Friar's denial, he replies angrily, 'How! Know you where you are?' (l. 289), and Ludowick responds in kind: 'Respect to your great place, and let the devil | Be sometime honoured fore his burning throne' (ll. 290–1). This elicits a hysterical outburst from the previously moderate Escalus: 'Why, thou unreverend and unhallowed friar... to th' rack with him. We'll touse you | Joint by joint' (5.1.302–8). To Caiaphas' rough questioning at the next tribunal reported by Matthew, 'What is the matter that these men witness against thee? I charge thee by the living God, that thou tell us, if thou be the Christ the Son of God' (26: 62–3), Jesus responds with a denial and a threat: 'Thou hast said it: nevertheless I say unto you, hereafter shall ye see the Son of man, sitting at the right hand of the power of God' (26: 64). This response is imitated by the Friar's cool disclosure of his special relation with the Duke: 'Be not so hot. The Duke | Dare no more stretch this finger of mine than he | Dare rack his own. His subject I am not' (5.1.310–12). Like Escalus, the high priest goes wild: '[he] rent his clothes, saying, "He hath blasphemed: what have we need of any more witnesses? What think ye?" They answered and said, "He is worthy to die"' (26: 65–6).

The Duke's false deputy, Angelo; his senior representative, Escalus; and his overt enemy, Lucio now join forces in the assault on his true deputy, the Friar. Lucio attributes his own scabrous allegations against the Duke to the Friar, who once again replaces a false substitution with a true one: 'You must, sir, change persons with me ere you make that my report' (5.1.333–4). The verbal attack becomes physical, and one would imagine that the watching stage crowd gets rowdy, while the theatre audience is excited by anticipation. Lucio starts to 'pluck [him] by the nose' (ll. 336–7), Escalus says, 'Lay bolts... upon him' (l. 343), and Angelo tells Lucio to help the officer. During the ensuing scuffle, first Lucio curses the Friar and then pulls at his hood: 'Why, you bald-pated lying rascal, you must be hooded, must you? ... Show your sheep-biting face, and be hanged an hour. Will't not off?' (5.1.349–52). Such a riotous climax also takes place before the gospel's high priest: 'Then spat they in his face, and buffeted him: and others smote him with their rods, saying "Prophesy to us, O Christ, who is he that smote thee?"' (Matt. 26: 67–8). And it continues after Jesus makes a similar appearance at the tribunal of Pilate 'as the crowd bowed their knees before him, and mocked him saying, "God save thee King of the Jews", and spitted upon him, and took a reed, and smote him on the head' (Matt. 27: 28–31). As in *Measure for Measure*, their mockery is mocked by the reader's knowledge that their victim is actually their ruler in disguise.

After Lucio pulls down his hood, everyone gasps in surprised recognition that the Friar is really the Duke. This is the primary dramatic climax of the play. It fulfils the purpose of his departure at the beginning, and of his several disguised returns: to reclaim a nation under sway of lawlessness, both by liberty and restraint. The conquering Vincentio triumphs over two formerly divided antagonists, now fully in league—Lucio and Angelo. Lucio tries to sneak away but is arrested. Angelo recognizes the omniscience of the Duke and admits his crime (5.1.367–70). Isabella prostrates herself and apologizes for his trouble.

The Duke reveals himself in the midst of chaos at the moment of his true deputy Ludowick's deepest humiliation. But it is a humiliation that he has engineered himself in every detail in order to 'make... heavenly comforts of despair | When [her good] is least expected' (4.3.107–8). All the members of his on-stage audience regard this revelation with surprise from their various vantages, while the reader or playgoer, who has been in on the preparations for the disclosure since the Duke's return, is gratified at the long-deferred resolution.

Likewise at the crucifixion, the gospel reaches its dramatic climax when God reveals himself at the moment of his true deputy's deepest humiliation:

Then Jesus cried again with a loud voice, and yielded up the ghost. And behold, the veil of the Temple was rent in twain, from the top to the bottom, and the earth did quake, and the stones were cloven, and the graves did open themselves, and many bodies of the saints which slept, arose, and came out of the graves after his resurrection, and went into the Holy City, and appeared unto many. When the Centurion, and they that were with him watching Jesus, saw... they feared greatly, saying, "Truly this was the Son of God."

(Matt. 27: 50–4)

As in Exodus, this revelation of God's power of deliverance is fore-warned—'Hereafter shall ye see the Son of man, sitting at the right hand of the power of God, and come in the clouds of the heaven' (Matt. 26: 64)—and its purposes are expounded in advance—'But all this was done, that the Scriptures of the Prophets might be ful-filled' (Matt. 26: 56). Typical of biblical narrative, such anticipation and explanation makes the climax seem both wondrous and stage-managed, a dazzling miracle framed by its own machinery.

The way Matthew reports it, the death of Jesus begins a process of resurrection that concludes three days later: 'there was a great earth-quake; the angel of the Lord... said... He is not here... for he has risen.... Behold Jesus also met them saying, "God save you"' (Matt. 28: 2, 6, 9–10). In *Measure for Measure*, a hundred lines after the Duke's unmasking, a third hooded figure is produced, unmasked, and resur-rected. Claudio has already died in several senses—to the attractions of life following the Friar's initial sermon, from the flesh into the spirit after his brief backslide, and to all those that knew and loved him who assumed that his head was sent to Angelo. Resurrection is itself a kind of unmasking or 'apocalypse', a prototype of the final revelation in the last book of the Bible that will conclude with all the dead coming back to life.

Measure for Measure concludes with this second narrative climax that dramatizes the gospel theme referred to by the play's title. Having indeed shown what happens when 'power change[s] purpose' and 'what our seemers be' (1.3.54), the Duke now concludes his effort to teach the truth to Isabella with a new batch of lies. No longer controlling her with scripted directions, Vincentio arranges for her freely to choose to forgo vengeance, even against his own mock insistence to the contrary. First he repeats that Claudio is dead and then condemns Angelo to die for killing him, 'Like doth quit like, and measure still for measure.... We do condemn thee to the very block | Where Claudio stooped to death' (5.1.408, 411–12). Both utterances tempt Isabella to find satisfaction in the punishment of her enemy—the 'justice' she demanded earlier and the 'revenges to your heart' promised by the Friar. The Duke here makes scriptural references in order to mislead, and misleads in order to teach the true path.

Pauline interpretation of the Bible attributes the same tactic to God. What he commanded in the Old Testament Law or Torah must now be superseded. Matthew's Jesus requires a repudiation of earlier biblical doctrines: 'You have heard that it hath been said "An eye for an eye and a tooth for a tooth," but I say unto you, "Resist not evil, but whosoever shall smite thee on thy right cheek, turn to him the other also... pray for them which hurt you and persecute you"' (5: 38, 44). Mariana follows this instruction by interceding with the Duke for her husband's life, and she begs Isabella to intercede for her, perhaps in the hope that like her own namesake Mary, who in Catholic tradition intercedes with Jesus to intercede for sinners, Isabella will lend the weight of her 'higher' wrongs to the appeal. The Duke refuses, secretly playing devil's advocate and threatening that if Isabella joins Mariana, Claudio's revenging ghost will take her to hell. But Mariana persists in asking forgiveness: 'They say best men are moulded out of faults, | And, for the most, become much more the better | For being a little bad' (5.1.436–8). This is the same reasoning with which Isabella had half-heartedly pleaded to Angelo, the reasoning he twisted into a demand for her body. But here, by pointed contrast, the underlying intent of the words is genuine. After a long pause, Isabella accedes and kneels next to Mariana, not only to beg for her enemy's life, but to argue as strenuously in Angelo's defence as she had in her brother's. Like Jesus on the cross who said, 'Forgive them: for they know not what they do' (Luke 23: 34), before the assembled multitude she now models the true forgiveness that leads her lord to 'find a way' to forgive those who have transgressed against him. But the play audience has been shown a secret still hidden from everyone else in Vienna. They have seen how the inner light which she now casts was kindled by the machinations of the Duke.

5

Accepting the benevolence of the Duke and experiencing the ending as happy may require a kind of orthodoxy, its very implausibility an exercise for the faithful. For Wilson Knight the play reflects the 'sublime strangeness and unreason of Jesus' teaching'.[19] Roy Battenhouse states that the play's real meaning is available only 'to members of the Christian guild, the story embodies the secret of their "craft;" it is their "mystery," calculated in its shrewd entertainment to scandalize some and mystify others. For those who understand it from within, it is absolutely normative in its art and its ethics.'[20] According to these critics, faith becomes the key to understanding Shakespeare's play, just as it is the key, according to Jesus, to understanding his symbolic parables. In line with such faith, orthodox interpreters read the Duke's final request for Isabella's hand as a representation of divine marriage—alternately symbolized in the New Testament as Jesus' union with the soul or God's marriage with the Church.[21]

But many readers find *Measure for Measure*'s supposedly comic ending untenable, either because they do not share the faith in the allegorized version, or because they think it overlooks the loveless and bitter quality of the three concluding marriages that are arranged by the Duke against the will of Angelo and Lucio and with Isabella's wordless acquiescence. However, the New Testament itself views earthly marriage as a compromise solution to the problem of controlling the flesh: 'It is good for a man not to touch a woman. Nevertheless, to avoid fornication, let every man have his wife, and let every woman have her own husband. ... if they cannot abide, let them marry: for it is better to marry than to burn' (1 Cor. 7: 1–2, 9). Paul's recommendations provide a pragmatic response to bodily promptings disastrously denied by Angelo and Isabella, overindulged by Lucio, and acknowledged by the Provost: 'All sects, all ages smack of this vice' (2.2.5).[22]

Another problem with the comic ending for non-orthodox readers resides in its apparent failure to resolve the original problems of 'government' plaguing the state of Vienna at the outset of the play. According to Leggatt, the Duke's 'solution does not work'.[23] However, in terms of the practical politics that Machiavelli might discover in biblical history, the Duke succeeds. The Duke's political goal, like the New Testament God's, is to re-establish lost authority over a community that has strayed from itself—that is, to achieve a reformation. Reformation entails repudiation of existing statutes, both ecclesiastical and secular, in order to strengthen government with the 'spirit' of voluntary compliance. Such compliance requires a political version of the spiritual faith that Jesus and Paul demand from their followers. While Henry V is patterned after the Hebrew Bible's holy warrior, who establishes power by 'busy[ing] giddy minds with foreign quarrels' (*2 Henry IV*, 4.3.342–3), Vincentio is modelled upon the New Testament pacifist leader who maintains his subjects' allegiance with surveillance, intimate appeals to conscience, and miraculous spectacles of punishment and forgiveness. In this respect, Duke Vincentio resembles Shakespeare's pacifist king, James I.[24]

Jesus' justification for indirection and misleading people—'they seeing do not see, and hearing, they hear not, neither understand' (Matt. 13: 13)—is echoed by Machiavelli's: 'men in general judge more by their eyes than their hands; for everyone can see but few can feel. Everyone sees what you seem to be, few touch upon what you are'.[25] King James, who described the monarch as a 'little God. . . . Resembling right your mighty King Divine', found in the biblical God's divine dissimulation an admirable model for worldly rulers.[26] His motto, *Qui nescit dissimulare, nescit regnare*—'He who does not know how to dissimulate does not know how to reign'[27]—could apply as well to the one whom Lucio calls the 'old fantastical Duke of dark corners' (4.3.152–3).

Like the God of the Bible, Vincentio triumphs over obstacles with what Machiavelli would consider a proper mixture of cruelty and mercy: 'Every prince must desire to be considered merciful and not cruel; nevertheless he must take care not to misuse this mercy.'[28] Too much mercy on the ruler's part will allow the people to run riot against one another and will undermine the sovereign's authority. Therefore 'it is much safer to be feared than to be loved'.[29] By appointing a deputy to enforce a crackdown and apparently leaving town, he can re-establish authority through fear and still retain the appearance of mercy: 'I have on Angelo imposed the office, | Who may in th'ambush of my name strike home, | And yet my nature never in the fight | T'allow in slander' (1.3.40–3).

However, the Duke knows from the start that his deputy is likely to fall into the trap that Machiavelli warns against: 'A prince must ... make himself feared in such a manner that he will avoid hatred, even if he does not acquire love; and this will always be so when he keeps his hands off the property and women of his citizens and his subjects.'[30] Angelo can't refrain from doing just that when he shuts down the bawdy houses and goes after Isabella.

The last act shows the Duke turning Angelo's failure to his own benefit with the drawn-out public spectacle of the hated deputy's self-exposure. Vincentio's comic political triumph parallels that of Cesare Borgia in Machiavelli's sardonic account of another Duke's political practice:

After the Duke had taken Romagna and found it governed by powerless lords ... so that the entire province was full of thefts, fights, and of every other kind of insolence, he decided that if he wanted to make it peaceful and obedient to the ruler's law, it would be necessary to give it good government. Therefore, he put Messer Remirro de Orco, a cruel and able man, in command there and gave him complete authority. This man, in little time made the province peaceful and united.... Afterwards, the Duke decided that such great authority was no longer required, for he was afraid that it might become odious; and he set up in the middle of the province a civil court.... And because he realised that the rigorous measures of the past had generated a certain amount of hatred, he wanted to show, in order to purge men's minds and to win them to his side completely, that if any form of cruelty had arisen, it did not originate from him but from the harsh nature of his minister. And having found the occasion to do this, one morning at Cesna he had Messer Remirro placed on the piazza in two pieces with a block of wood and a bloody sword beside him. The ferocity of such a spectacle left those people satisfied and amazed at the same time.[31]

In the New Testament, Angelo's role of merciless, legalistic, hypocritical, and obdurate deputy belongs to the Pharisees. They provide no forgiveness of sins, they torment the guiltless, they persecute their own disguised Lord, and when confronted, they fail to confess their crimes and acknowledge his authority. Though they are not chopped into two pieces like Messer Remirro, the ferocity of condemnation heaped upon them, as upon Angelo, leaves later readers of the Bible 'satisfied and amazed at the same time'. The Duke's political success in setting up Angelo as his enforcer and then repudiating him suggests that Shakespeare may have perceived the same successful political strategy working in the Christian Bible's use of the Jews.

In addition to Angelo, the other antagonist exposed at the end of *Measure for Measure* is Lucio. The Luciferian adversary who joined forces with the fallen Angelo to attack the Friar is also spared from the deserved death penalty but forced to join into the community of marriage under the regenerated regime of the returned Duke. Likewise the scribes, priests, and other Jews who share in the persecution of Jesus are both demonized and interceded for. And while insisting that God has rejected the Jews in favour of Christians, Paul also prophesies their eventual 'grafting in' again to the community of the faithful (Rom. II: II–26).

Nevertheless, Angelo makes no acknowledgement of his pardon or of Mariana's love, and Lucio, rather than gratefully accepting the grace extended to him, responds with an irreverent jest implying that the Duke's divine return is nothing more than an act: 'Your highness said even now I made you a duke; good my lord, do not recompense me in making me a cuckold' (5.1.515–16). Similarly, after the resurrection, the chief priests and elders are reported to pay Roman soldiers to bear false witness that the disciples stole the body from the tomb to support the Jews' continuing claims that the resurrection was a hoax (Matt. 28: II–15). Just as the reader of the Bible knows that these Jews are liars, the reader of *Measure for Measure* knows that Lucio's discrediting of the Duke is false. And yet, given the shifting religious, political, and theatrical grounds upon which borders between falsehood and truth are determined, the only lines one can draw with full confidence are parallels.[32]

| 6

'Dangerous Conceits' and 'Proofs of Holy Writ': Allusion *in* The Merchant of Venice *and Paul's Letter to the Romans*

I

The Merchant of Venice was written about eight years before *Measure for Measure*, during the reign of King James's predecessor, Queen Elizabeth. However, in the First Folio's collection of Shakespeare's plays, it is situated among the comedies, several plays after *Measure for Measure*. Likewise, though Paul's epistles were written a generation before the four gospels and the Acts of the Apostles, which recorded the events in Jesus' and Paul's lives, those letters were positioned after the first five books by the editors of the New Testament. Paul's epistle to the Romans explores the relationship between Jews and Christians in the course of a theological reflection on the significance of events recorded in the Hebrew Bible and later in the four gospels. *The Merchant of Venice* explores the relationship between Jews and Christians in the course of a dramatized reflection on the Hebrew and Christian Bibles and on the process of biblical allusion by which their influence is expressed in this and other Shakespeare plays.

As in *Measure for Measure*, in *The Merchant of Venice* Shakespeare seems to work with two kinds of sources. Plots and characters from

Italian prose fictions are blended with frequent allusions and parallels to the Bible—perhaps mediated by the tradition of English liturgical mystery drama. The conflict between villainous Jew and virtuous Christians at the centre of the story appears in the secular sources, where the Jew fills the role of comic butt, but in none of those are the biblical parallels of this conflict elaborated. By expanding them, Shakespeare theologizes the comedy and renders theology as entertainment.

Like *Measure for Measure* and its gospel models, *The Merchant of Venice* attains its dramatic climax in a long, suspenseful trial sequence at the end of which the accuser stands accused and the ideal of loving mercy ostensibly triumphs over the corrupt standard of harsh justice in a 'comedy of forgiveness'. And yet, to many, this outcome seems questionable or ironic. Like *Measure for Measure*, *The Merchant of Venice* is therefore often classified as a 'problem play', one which incongruously superimposes tragic patterns upon comic ones, and which generates contrary critical and performance interpretations.

The Merchant of Venice contains more biblical allusions than any other play by Shakespeare.[1] Allusion is usefully defined as a device whereby a speaker or writer 'explicitly activat[es] an earlier text as part of the new system of meaning and aesthetic value of his own text'.[2] Allusion takes place at two levels. One is among characters on stage. They may refer to the Bible simply because its phraseology is so widely embedded in the language of their culture, or they may do it purposefully. In the first scene Graziano says to Antonio, 'You have too much respect upon the world. | They lose it that do buy it with much care' (1.1.74–5). His proverbial remark echoes Matthew 16: 26—'For what is a man profited if he shall win the whole world, and lose his own Soul?' The allusion is intended to comfort, flatter, and amuse the older man both with piety and with wit. As the play continues, Graziano's allusions express his habitual efforts to please by mixing righteousness and profanity.

Shylock also fashions himself with biblical allusion. This is an aspect of his identification with 'our people', the Jews, known by Renaissance Europeans as 'people of the book'. His 'ancient grudge' against Christians is expressed by a mocking reference to the gospel account of Jesus exorcizing demons into the Gadarene swine (1.3.31–2). He tells a lengthy version of the Genesis story of Jacob tricking Laban

first level of allusion through character

with sharp business practice, not only to justify his own collection of interest but to link himself with the namesake of the nation of Israel (1.3.70–89).

The second level of allusion activates meanings at the level of communication between author and audience, a level outside the awareness of the characters. Shakespeare uses allusion to link his characters and their biblical namesakes: Leah, Shylock's dead wife, with Jacob's first wife; Jessica, his daughter, with Lot's sister; Chus and Tubal, his associates, with Noah's sons. Or he portrays them with traits and in situations that point to such linkages—for instance, Antonio before the knife-wielding Shylock as a sacrificial Christ brought to the slaughter. In doing so Shakespeare prompts his reader to think of differences as well as similarities between them. For example, unbeknownst to Graziano, his biblical references to Jesus' words about worldliness reveal the tendency he shares with his friends to confuse the religious ideal of contempt for this world with the aristocratic affectation of contempt for money.

With what Robert Alter refers to as 'global allusion', an author can also activate larger plot lines and patterns from an earlier work:

> I would prefer to call this sort of global allusion 'midrashic', remembering the tendency of the early rabbis in the Midrash to interpret Scripture by fleshing it out, recreating it in contemporary narrative terms. Midrashic allusion is generated when one writer is under the spell of an earlier one, whether happily or not.... [It] is an exegetical meditation through narration on a potent earlier text.[3]

The play's story of rivalry between Venetian Jews and Christians recalls the rivalries between Jews and Christians recorded throughout the New Testament,[4] as well as in the editing and commentaries of the Christian version of the Hebrew Bible, the Old Testament. With this global allusion, Shakespeare himself undertakes 'an exegetical meditation through narration' on that topic.

For a reader, allusion often promises a key to decipher a code that makes sense out of otherwise incomprehensible, inconsistent, or unacceptable portions of the surface text. It leads to a secret subtext that is actually a prior text interpreted in a certain way. Allusion thereby creates a feeling of intimacy and heightened communication between reader and author, reader and text, or reader and the interpretative community which shares the key—in the words of Iago, 'confirmations strong | As proofs of holy writ' (*Othello*, 3.3.327–8).

However, because its messages cross so many gaps of association and translation, allusion can also function to subvert meaning and 'overwrite' an original text by means of selective quotation, distortion, and tendentious or biased interpretation. It can easily create misunderstanding and misreading. For Richard of Gloucester it becomes a tool of political manipulation:

> But then I sigh, and with a piece of scripture
> Tell them that God bids us do good for evil;
> And thus I clothe my naked villainy
> With odd old ends, stol'n forth of Holy Writ,
> And seem a saint when most I play the devil.
> (*Richard III*, 1.3.331–6)

Manipulated in this fashion, as Iago observes, 'Trifles light as air' can produce 'Dangerous conceits' (*Othello* 3.3.326, 330).

Alter's definition of 'global allusion' concludes, 'the older text is not just something the poet reads but something that possesses him, and the re-creation of the old work in the new is an effort to make sense of that experience of possession, to explain what cultural memory means'.[5] Similarly, a reader's inclination is to thrill in breaking the code of allusion and to glory in sharing secrets reserved for the chosen. But upon reflection, the reader may seek release from the 'possession' that such discovery produces. Shakespeare dramatized these tendencies in his characters, in his readers, and in readers of the Bible. In addition to an exegetical meditation, *The Merchant of Venice* is Shakespeare's 'effort to make sense of that experience of possession, to explain what cultural memory means'. Part of the explanation he found was that allusion itself is the method by which the authors of the Christian Bible took possession of the Hebrew Bible, the 'potent earlier text' they meditated upon and activated as part of their new system of meaning. By repeatedly revealing the contingent and ambiguous nature of biblical allusion in sixteenth-century Venice, Shakespeare may also have meant to suggest something about its use by the earliest Christians.

The Merchant of Venice's harsh portrayal of religious and ethnic hostility continues to provoke strong defensive reactions. D. M. Cohen remarks upon 'the fear and shame that Jewish viewers have always felt' when exposed to its stereotyped portrait of Shylock's hard 'Jewish heart' (4.1.79) and to the vicious anti-Semitic curses that are heaped upon him.[6] The memory of the Nazi holocaust has also made many non-Jews uneasy about this work. Even if Shakespeare did not subscribe to the attitudes of his characters, 'It is as though *The Merchant of Venice* is an anti-Semitic play written by an author who is not an anti-Semite—but an author who has been willing to use the cruel stereotypes of that ideology for mercenary and artistic purposes.'[7] How one construes the play's biblical allusions seems hard to separate from what one feels about Judaism in general, and many, though by no means all, ironic readings of the play have been formulated by commentators with Jewish names: Berger, Levin, Bloom, Fiedler. James Shapiro has located *The Merchant of Venice* within the history of English anti-Semitism, exploring its cultural roots, showing how it functioned historically to strengthen the definition of English identity as essentially non-Jewish, citing a number of present-day expressions of disapproval regarding the prominence of Jews among contemporary Shakespearians.[8] Part of my own agenda in this chapter is to dispute traditional invidious comparisons between the Hebrew and Christian Bibles that have been discredited by modern biblical scholars but which occasionally still are reinforced by literary critics.

2

In a widely cited study, Barbara Lewalski sets out to uncover in *The Merchant of Venice* 'patterns of biblical allusion and imagery so precise and pervasive as to be patently deliberate'. Following a line of interpretation first proposed by Sir Israel Gollancz and further developed by Nevill Coghill, she reads it as a kind of *Divine Comedy*, to be interpreted according to the medieval allegorical method of reading Scripture. The joyous marriages at the end stand for the divine marriage at the end of the book of Revelation, the tribulations of the lovers represent the struggles of the faithful, while the antagonist Shylock represents Satan and his minions, the Jews. Jews and devils are identified nine times in the play just as Christ links them in John's gospel and elsewhere.[9]

Antonio is represented as 'the very embodiment of Christian love, and Shylock functions as one ... antithesis to it'.[10] Antonio's carelessness regarding things of this world is founded upon a trust in God's providence. His self-forgetfulness and humility is based on recognition of man's common sinfulness. For the sake of love, he is ready to give and risk everything, willing to forgive injuries and embrace enemies. Shylock, on the other hand, stands for 'thrift'. His watch words are, 'Fast bind, fast find' (2.5.53), applied both to his daughter and his ducats. He is materialistic, proud, and self righteous, and he disdains simplicity, festivity, and music.

The confrontation between Shylock and Antonio, according to Lewalski, represents the juxtaposition of Judaism and Christianity as theological systems—old law and new—and as historic societies. With a reference to the parable of the Pharisee and publican in Luke 18: 9–13, Shylock identifies himself as a member of the chosen people and scorns Antonio as a profane Gentile (1.3.39–40). His fallacious biblical justification for usury is refuted by Antonio with a reference to the Aristotelian and Thomistic argument against usury, echoing that of Jesus in the gospels.

The rivalry between Christian and Jew comes to a head in the trial scene in Act 4, Scene 1, where numerous biblical allusions tie this incident to the trial scenes in the four gospels that expose an innocent Jesus to the cruelty of the Jews. While Shylock clamours for revenge, the Duke and Portia beg him for mercy, alluding both to the prescription in the Lord's Prayer for forgiveness and to Jesus' request that one love one's enemies and turn one's other cheek to one's oppressors. This is what Antonio does while he is being arraigned and once Shylock is at his mercy. Shylock, by contrast, says, 'My deeds upon my head' (4.1.203), associating himself with the brutal, self-incriminating words of the Jews in the gospels: 'His blood be on us and our children' (Matt. 27: 25).

Shylock arrogates righteousness to himself: 'What judgement shall I dread, doing no wrong?' (4.1.88). His insistence that 'I stand for judgement' (l. 102), or 'I stand here for law' (l. 141), is set against Portia's earlier statement, 'I stand for sacrifice' (3.2.57). This opposition resembles the contrast of law and works versus love and faith that marks the theological difference between Judaism and Christianity, according to Paul's letter to the Romans.

Portia arrives to defend Antonio, cloaked in biblical allusions. She is disguised as 'Balthasar', a name given to the prophet Daniel when he comes to defend the Jews in the court of the Babylonian king. Shylock refers to her as 'A Daniel come to judgement' (4.1.220), thinking she represents his position. Once she turns the tables on him, Graziano mockingly repeats this epithet, now referring to the 'second Daniel' (4.1.330) in the apocryphal addition to the book of Daniel, who turned the tables on the guilty elders after they falsely accused Susanna.[11] Finally, the way Portia construes the law that justifies Shylock so that it condemns him alludes to St Paul's claim that the law with which the Jews justify themselves will condemn them: 'Therefore by the works of the Law shall no flesh be justified in his sight: for by the Law cometh the knowledge of sin' (Rom. 3: 20).

Another pattern of allusion to Romans is found in the outcome of the trial. After being defeated by the law, Shylock is condemned to death, and his wealth is conferred upon the Christians of the city. Paul's reading of biblical history follows the same pattern: 'I demand then, have they stumbled, that they should fall? God forbid: but through their fall salvation cometh unto the Gentiles, to provoke them [the Jews] to follow them' (Rom. 11: 12). Shylock the Jew has lost his riches both to his daughter Jessica who has run off to Belmont with Christian Lorenzo and also to Antonio and the city of Venice to whom he must forfeit all that is left. However, Antonio graciously asks mercy for the condemned Jew with the proviso that he convert to Christianity, pay a fine, and give half his fortune to Antonio for use during his lifetime and the other half to Jessica upon his death. Shylock consents, thereby fulfilling the Pauline prophecy.

According to Lewalski, the biblical allusions assure that this outcome is meant to be fully comic: 'thus the stipulation for Shylock's conversion . . . is not anti-semitic revenge: it simply compels Shylock to avow what his own experience in the trial scene has fully "demonstrated"—that the Law leads only to death and destruction, that faith in Christ must supplant human righteousness'.[12]

Though the play's other plot line, the courtship of Bassanio and Portia, exhibits no obvious biblical allusion, Lewalski finds significant parallels. Bassanio triumphs over his competitors for Portia's hand in the casket scene because he is willing to hazard all for love, like Antonio and a follower of Christ throwing concern for self to the winds and trusting to faith. The choice itself is presented in language echoing the choice for or against God offered by Moses at the end of

[handwritten margin note: Pattern of allusion to BK of Romans trial scene]

Deuteronomy. Bassanio's rejection of the silver or gold exterior shows his rejection of wealth and pride in favour of humility and true love: 'Bassanio's choice of the lead casket is the choice of life, the love of God.'[13]

Lewalski claims that biblical allusion yields a parallel between Christ's sacrifice and Bassanio's willingness to sacrifice everything after the defeat of Shylock—'life itself, my wife, and all the world' (4.1.281)—for the love of Antonio, who pressures him into giving away his engagement ring. This betrayal of his fiancée is also a sign of Bassanio's human frailty and need for forgiveness. After having been put through a trial and interrogation by Portia in the final scene, like everybody else, he is forgiven for not measuring up to his own obligations to his highest love. The play concludes in the 'Heavenly City' of Belmont with the delivery of riches—to Antonio through the rescue of his merchant ships, to Bassanio and Graziano through marriage to wealthy women, and to Lorenzo and Jessica through the grant of Shylock's estate. Though Jesus and Paul associated the pursuit of wealth with greedy Jews and saw it as inimical to a Christian way of life, both Christians and Jews in *The Merchant of Venice* are always concerned with money. So a distinction is required. According to C. L. Barber, 'the whole play dramatizes the conflict between the mechanisms of wealth and the masterful, social use of it'.[14]

Thus global biblical allusions, with special emphasis on the epistle to the Romans, provide *The Merchant of Venice* with a coherent religious, moral, and dramatic interpretation. According to Frank Kermode:

> *The Merchant of Venice* is 'about' judgement, redemption and mercy; the supersession in human history of the grim four thousand years of unalleviated justice by the era of love and mercy. It begins with usury and corrupt love; it ends with harmony and perfect love. And all the time it tells its audience that this is its subject; only by a determined effort to avoid the obvious can one mistake the theme of *The Merchant of Venice*.[15]

3

Despite such insistence, many actors and critics have responded to the play differently. A tradition of reading against the grain of biblical allegory extends back to William Hazlitt in the early nineteenth century. Such readings pursue a 'hermeneutic of suspicion' that mistrusts the play's apparent divisions into heroes and villains who embody the dominant society's divisions of honour and blame. Instead they highlight ways the text critiques and reverses orthodox hierarchy.

The notion that the romantic courtships of the play represent a divine comedy of love between God and humanity is undermined by the fact that all three males are shown as fortune hunters and all three females as social climbers. Richard A. Levin observes that in *The Merchant of Venice*, love and marriage privilege those with status, money, and power, while the losers are all outsiders. The traditional handsome hero and charming heroine 'forfeit our sympathy' in their victory over their stage-villain antagonist because of their calculating ways of courting and their purchase of success by the loss of others.[16] Rather than 'figur[ing] forth a Heavenly City'[17] or a romantic fairyland of music and beauty that contrasts with the self-seeking mercantile world of Venice, Belmont is a country-club suburb which excludes Jews, homosexuals, and foreigners of any complexion, disguising its own cutthroat competition for status and control with surface gentility.

Levin asserts that Christians trade love and money no less greedily, if a little more subtly, than the Jews. Bassanio needs to borrow money to court Portia whom he values first for her money. Antonio attempts to buy Bassanio's love with his money. The Duke tells Bassanio to pay off Balthasar the judge with money. Jessica and Lorenzo elope with the stolen money of her father and counter his thrift not with generosity but prodigality. Just as Shylock wagers his three thousand ducats for Antonio's pound of flesh, Graziano bets one thousand ducats that he and Nerissa will have a male baby before Bassanio and Portia (3.2.213–14). The real God of both Christians and Jews in Venice and Belmont is Fortune—in both senses of the word.[18]

Rather than the saintly self-sacrificing lover she claims to be when she 'converts' her father's legacy to Bassanio, Portia is a canny and conniving sophisticate whose holy words and gestures do not always correspond to her underlying motives. When we first meet her she acknowledges the distance between good intentions and virtuous behaviour (1.2.12–20). She rejects one of her suitors with words preferring fleshly appearance to spiritual essence: 'If he have the condition of a saint and the complexion of a devil, I had rather he should shrive me than wive me' (1.2.126–8). And she lies irreverently about with-drawing to a convent—'I have toward heaven breathed a secret vow | To live in prayer and contemplation' (3.4.27–8)—as an alibi for dressing up as a man and spying on her fiancé.

Antonio and Shylock may be antagonists, but they also have much in common. Despite their wealth, Levin observes, both are socially marginal—Shylock because he is Jewish, and Antonio because (like the Antonio of *Twelfth Night*) he is hopelessly in love with another man who is about to marry. Like the other racial and national aliens mocked by Portia and Nerissa, they both end up as excluded from the festivity at the end of the play.

Though Shylock's conversion may allude to Paul's prediction of the Jews' 'acceptance' as signalling 'Nothing less than life from the dead' (Rom. 11: 15), its portrayal here does not display much change of heart. He agrees to become a Christian because it is the only alternative to a death sentence, and upon accepting he says, 'I pray you give me leave to go from hence. I am not well' (4.1.392). His daughter Jessica converts only because of social pressure. Though applauded for doing it by Lorenzo, her Christian fiancé and beneficiary, she feels guilty: 'what heinous sin is it in me | To be ashamed to be my father's child!... I shall end this strife, | Become a Christian and thy loving wife' (2.3.16–21).

And as a converted Jewess, she is still open to the mistrust and ridicule of the Gentiles: 'He tells me flatly there's no mercy for me in heaven because I am a Jew's daughter, and he says you are no good member of the commonwealth, for in converting Jews to Christians you raise the price of pork' (3.5.30–4). For Shylock's servant, Launcelot Gobbo, leaving his master and joining the Christians is represented as both a liberation and a betrayal: 'To be ruled by my conscience I should stay with the Jew my master who, God bless the mark, is a kind of devil; and to run away from the Jew I should be ruled by the fiend who, saving your reverence, is the devil himself' (2.2.20–4).

In contrast to harsh Jewish justice, Antonio, Portia, and the Duke claim the mantle of loving Christian mercy: 'That thou shalt see the difference of our spirit, | I pardon thee thy life before thou ask it' (4.1.365–6). But once Shylock loses his case, Graziano gleefully demands his death. It remains questionable whether the sentence of forced conversion (often handed down to European Jews) is merciful

or vengeful, but Shakespeare earlier allowed Shylock a lengthy statement of his own point of view on the issue of vengeance:

If you prick us do we not bleed? If you tickle us do we not laugh? If you poison
us do we not die? And if you wrong us shall we not revenge? If we are like you
in the rest, we will resemble you in that. If a Jew wrong a Christian, what is his
humility? Revenge. If a Christian wrong a Jew, what should his sufferance be
by Christian example? Why revenge. The villainy you teach me I will execute,
and it shall go hard but I will better the instruction.   (3.1.59–68)

Réne Girard reads this speech as authoritative:

Between Shylock's behaviour and his words, the relationship is never ambiguous. . . . In the passage on revenge, he alone speaks a truth that the Christians
hypocritically deny. The truth of the play is revenge and retribution. The
Christians manage to hide that truth even from themselves. They do not live
by the law of charity, but this law is enough of a presence in their language to
drive the law of revenge underground, to make this revenge almost invisible. . . . The Christians will easily destroy Shylock but they will go on living in
a world that is sad without knowing why, a world in which even the difference
between revenge and charity has been abolished.[19]

4

The persistence of such opposed interpretations has prompted Norman Rabkin to use *The Merchant of Venice* as his primary example of
'the problem of meaning' in all Shakespeare's work. He concludes that
it is not 'about' any one theme, but rather the play of contradictory
meanings and messages in both its characters and its audience:

The best reading and the best production . . . would have to take account of the
possibilities of both readings . . . by the end we have been through a constantly
turbulent experience which demands an incessant giving and taking back of
allegiance, a counterpoint of ever-shifting response to phrase, speech, character, scene, action . . . the power of the play is its power to create the illusion of
a life that is like our lives . . . in which . . . experience tempts us to believe itself
to be reducible to fundamental terms but cannot be adequately analyzed in
those terms.[20]

This description could apply to drama in general, where a multiplicity
of viewpoints is always presented. But it is especially fitting for works
that prominently feature allusion. Allusion's meanings are generated

across a kind of synapse between the earlier and later work. In isolating an expression from its original context, it opens a range of meanings in its new context, rendering that expression symbolic, suggestive, and indeterminate—in Rabkin's words, 'turbulent' or 'contrapuntal'. It allows the writer to control the meaning of the evoked text and the reader to control the meaning of the alluding one.

Allusion is often pious. It can amplify the later utterance by asso- ciating it with a prestigious forerunner text, by providing authoritative evidence to support a given point, by echoing a memorable expression, or by stimulating a mysterious sensation of *déjà vu*. Portia's speech pleading for mercy from Shylock takes on oracular sanctity because of extended resonance with scriptural passages: 'The quality of mercy is not strained. | It droppeth as the gentle rain from heaven | Upon the place beneath' (4.1.181–3) recalls Ecclesiasticus 35: 19, 'O how fair a thing is mercy in the time of anguish and trouble? It is like a cloud of rain that cometh in the time of drought'. And Deuteronomy 32: 2, 'My doctrine shall drop as the rain and my speech shall [di] stil as doeth the dew, as the shower upon the herbs, and as the great rain upon the grass'. Portia's 'It is an attribute to God Himself' (l. 192) recalls Ecclesiasticus 2: 21, 'For his mercy is as great as himself'. Her 'Though justice be thy plea, consider this: | That in the course of justice none of us | Should see salvation' (ll. 195–7) refers to Psalm 143: 2, 'Enter not into judgement with thy servants, O Lord, for no flesh is righteous in thy sight.' Her 'We do pray for mercy, | And that same prayer doth teach us all to render | The deeds of mercy' (ll. 197–9) refers to the Lord's Prayer, 'Forgive us our debts, as we also forgive our debtors' (Matt. 6: 12) and to its source in Ecclesiasticus: 'Forgive thy neighbour the hurt that he hath done thee, and so shall thy sins be forgiven thee also when thou prayest' (28: 2–4).

Allusion can also subvert the original meaning of an activated text by placing it in a new context. Bassanio, for example, alludes to Proverbs—'As for favour, it is deceitful, and beauty is a vain thing' (31: 30)—as he contemplates his choice among the three caskets: 'Look on beauty | And you shall see 'tis purchased by the weight ... Making them lightest that wear most of it' (3.2.88–91). But as he speaks, Bassanio is struggling to find the most beautiful of women, whose golden portrait he will soon discover as a prize inside the leaden box. Replying to Bassanio's earlier dinner invitation, Shylock alludes subversively to the story of Jesus exorcizing demons and sending them from people into swine (Mark 5: 1–13, Luke 8: 26–33): 'Yes, to smell pork, to eat of the habitation which your prophet the Nazarite conjured the devil into!' (1.3.31–3). This reference identifies Christian loathing of demons with his own Jewish loathing of pork.

A third kind of allusion is ironic. It activates the earlier text as if to invoke its prestige and pay it homage, but other cues reveal sarcasm. Portia upbraids herself with an allusion to Romans: 'For the good which I would do I do not; but the evil which I would not, that do I' (7: 18–19). But she follows it up with an endless litany of proverbs to the same effect, rendering the expression as self-consuming as the sentiment it expresses: 'If to do were as easy as to know what were good to do, chapels had been churches, and poor men's cottages princes' palaces. It is a good divine that follows his own instructions. I can easier teach twenty what were good to be done than be one of the twenty to follow mine own teaching' (1.2.12–17). Launcelot Gobbo warns Jessica that she will be damned as a Jew despite her conversion because 'the sins of the father are to be laid upon the children' (3.5.1–2). This reference to Exodus 20: 5 is jocular in the first place, it mocks the fundamental distinction between ethnic Judaism and faith-centred Christianity, and it ridicules the Calvinist theology of predestination. Shakespeare's villains, clowns, and figures of misrule often use ironic allusion either to mock the scriptural text itself or those whose speech is loaded with pious allusion. In *Twelfth Night*, drunk Sir Toby Belch alludes to Paul's rejection of works as a path to salvation: 'Let him be the devil an he will, I care not. Give me faith, say I' (1.5.123–4). Falstaff alludes to Paul's injunction to work for a living (1 Cor. 7: 20 and Eph. 4: 1) to justify his activity as a robber: ''tis my vocation, Hal. 'Tis no sin for a man to labour in his vocation' (*1 Henry IV*, 1.2.104–5). This comes shortly after he has piously accused Hal of just such blasphemous use of Scripture: 'O, thou hast damnable iteration, and art indeed able to corrupt a saint' (1.2.90–1). In *A Midsummer Night's Dream*, Bottom the weaver recollects his transformation to an ass who made love to the Queen of the Fairies: 'The eye of man hath not heard, the ear of man hath not seen, man's hand is not able to taste, his tongue to conceive, nor his heart to report what my dream was' (4.1.208–11). These malapropisms parody St Paul's account of union with God: 'The eye hath not seen and the ear hath not heard neither have entered into the heart of man, the things which God hath prepared for them that love him' (1 Cor. 1: 9).

However, Bottom's ironic biblical allusion may also suggest piety by translating his grotesque experience into a real epiphany appropriate to his station and time. Conversely, the pious allusion of Portia may be slightly ironic, in that it actually derives from the Jewish Apocrypha and the Hebrew Bible. And Shylock's subversive allusion includes sarcasm by reducing Jesus from the Son of God to 'your prophet the Nazarite' (1.3.32). Pious, subversive, and ironic meanings 'demand an incessant giving and taking back of allegiance'.[21]

Shylock's sarcastic comment prompts Antonio to respond: 'Mark ... Bassanio? | The devil can cite Scripture for his purpose.... O, what a goodly outside falsehood hath!' (1.3.96–7, 101). Here he calls attention to the play's thematic concern with biblical allusion, above and beyond its actual uses of allusion. Antonio's warning about allusion is itself a biblical allusion to familiar passages in Matthew (4: 5) and Luke (4: 10) where Satan tempts Jesus with biblical references that Jesus overtops with other biblical references.

This allusion, piously intended, aligns Christian Antonio with Jesus against devilish Shylock in the competitive exchange of biblical allusions that continues in the gospel accounts of Jesus' later debates with the Jews. But the self-reflexive warning about quoting Scripture for unholy purposes does not apply only to devils and Jews. Bassanio, the hero, utters a similar caution as he wonders which text marks the casket that will win him wife and fortune, and which will lead him astray: 'In religion, | What damnèd error but some sober brow | Will bless it and approve it with a text, | Hiding the grossness with fair ornament?' (3.2.77–80).

He too moralizes upon the deceptiveness of the most sanctified and authoritative words, the 'dangerous conceits' in 'proofs of Holy Writ'. At this point, however, Bassanio is taking the cue for this observation from the words of the song that Portia has played while he deliberates:

> Tell me where is fancy bred,
> . . . . . .
> It is engendered in the eyes,
> With gazing fed; and fancy dies
> In the cradle where it lies,

> Let us all ring fancy's knell.
> I'll begin it: Ding, dong, bell.
> (3.2.63, 67–71)

These pious lyrics, which hint that all that glisters is not gold or silver, secretly convey the correct answer to the riddle of the caskets to Bassanio. They work the same kind of sharp practice for love and money that Jacob and Rachel carried out on Laban. The whole scene of selecting the 'chosen' Christian over Muslims, Turks, and other outsiders might recall the reply of Jesus to the disciples who ask why he speaks in riddling parables: 'To you it is given to know the mystery of the kingdom of God: but unto them that are without, all things be done in parables, that they seeing, may see, and not discern: and they hearing, may hear, and not understand, lest at any time they should turn, and their sins should be forgiven them' (Mark 4: 11–12).

Adapted from Isaiah 6: 9, this passage is reiterated throughout the New Testament—at Matthew 13: 14, Luke 8: 10, John 12: 40, Acts 28: 26, and Romans 11: 8. Jesus' insistence on the exclusivity of comprehension creates a community of privileged initiates in those who follow him. Those who fail to get the message are eternally damned:

For unto every man that hath, it shall be given, and he shall have abundance, and from him that hath not, even that he hath, shall be taken away. Cast therefore that unprofitable servant into utter darkness: there shall be weeping and gnashing of teeth.... Then shall he say unto them on the left hand, 'Depart from me ye cursed, into everlasting fire which is prepared for the devil and his angels.' (Matt. 25: 29–30, 41)

Or as John put it, 'Ye are of your father the devil ... He that is of God, heareth God's words: ye therefore hear them not, because ye are not of God' (John 8: 44–7).

Modern theologians refer to such passages as 'hard sayings' and are troubled by their inconsistency with the claim that Christ is a God of forgiveness rather than vengeance, a claim supportable only with selective quotation. That Shakespeare also noticed the New Testament's mixture of kindness and harshness is made clear in the allusions to Matt. 19: 14 and 24 that he puts into the mouth of *Richard II*:

> As thoughts of things divine, are intermixed
> With scruples, and do set the faith itself

> Against the faith, as thus: 'Come, little ones',
> And then again,
> 'It is as hard to come as for a camel
> To thread the postern of a small needle's eye.'
> (5.5.12–17)

When the playwright has Shylock accuse Christians of being as human and therefore as vengeful as Jews, he may refer not only to Shylock's fellow Venetians but also to their biblical teachers.

Bassanio warns against lawyers as well as theologians: 'In law, what plea so tainted and corrupt | But, being seasoned with a gracious voice, | Obscures the show of evil?' (3.2.75–7). His observation applies to Shylock's insistence that the court enforce his murderous contract with Antonio, and by extension to the way Paul characterizes the Jews' use of the law: 'Behold thou art called a Jew, and restest in the Law, and gloriest in God . . . Thou that gloriest in the Law, through breaking the Law dishonourest thou God?' (2: 17, 23).

However, in pleading for Antonio, Portia also uses strenuous legalisms. One of the two arguments that win over the judges redefines the penalty agreed to by Antonio as a fleshly sacrifice that is to be bloodless and perfectly precise—a sacrifice impossible to offer or exact (4.1.321–9). Likewise, Paul drains the traditional redemption value out of Jewish blood rituals such as circumcision and temple offerings because of their failure to manifest purity of spirit and faith: 'For circumcision verily is profitable, if thou dost do the Law: but if thou be a transgressor of the Law, thy circumcision is made uncircumcision. Therefore if the uncircumcision [*sic*] keep the ordinances of the Law, shall not his uncircumcision be counted for circumcision?' (2:25–6)

Portia's second legal strategy is to invoke a law hitherto unknown to Shylock and the judges that protects Venetian citizens from attacks by aliens in their midst (4.1.343–59). Though discovering a statute that is selectively applied seems the opposite of Paul's endeavour to universalize the sectarian Jewish covenant between God and his chosen people, the new community he organizes may be seen to exclude anyone who does not share beliefs in justification by faith and the resurrection of Christ. In that sense, Portia's new law may resemble his new covenant.

The bitter-tasting comic outcome of Shylock's forced conversion resembles Paul's tentative prophecy of the Jews' future reconciliation with God and the Gentiles: 'Have they stumbled that they should fall? God forbid: but through their fall salvation cometh unto the Gentiles, to provoke them to follow them' (11:11). '[P]artly obstinacy is come to Israel until the fullness of the Gentiles be come in. And so all Israel shall be saved ... As concerning the Gospel, they are enemies for your sakes: but as touching the election, they are beloved for the fathers' sakes' (11: 25–6, 28).

For Shakespeare's Christians, the triumph realized in the legal defeat and forced conversion of the Jew is accompanied by a financial windfall. The monetary aspect of the fortunate outcome echoes the terms of Paul's metaphor for the equivalent victory:

Wherefore if the fall of [the Jews] be the riches of the world, and the diminishing of them the riches of the Gentiles, how much more shall their abundance be. ... Behold therefore the bountifulness and severity of God: toward them which have fallen, severity; but toward thee, bountifulness, if thou continue in his bountifulness: or else thou shalt also be cut off.

(Rom. 11: 12, 22)

A reference to this transfer of wealth returns at the play's end, as the Jew's bounty falls into the waiting Christian hands of Lorenzo, brought not by God but the benefactors of Belmont: 'Fair ladies, you drop manna in the way | Of starvèd people' (5.1.293–4). The allusion to manna here may be a pious expression of gratitude for God's deliverance with a reference to Jesus' own sacrifice: 'This is the bread, which cometh down from heaven, that he which eateth of it, should not die' (John 6: 50). But Lorenzo's piety is usually ironic, for example when he jokes with Graziano that Jessica is 'true' at the very moment that she is betraying her father and he is playing 'thieves for wives' (2.6.23, 55). His allusion to manna here, then, also expresses a mercenary joy at finding a bonanza, like a Las Vegas winner's declaration that 'there is a God'. And in its original Old Testament contexts, the dropping of manna has an intrinsically ironic meaning that could rankly spoil the happy ending. In Exodus 16, the Israelites hoard the manna which God grants them for subsistence, and it turns into maggots. In Numbers 11: 6 they complain that manna is not enough, so God sends them quail poisoned with the plague (11:33).

5

The struggle of competing meanings among these pious, subversive, and ironic allusions to manna is partly a matter of Old versus New Testament references. The struggle over Shylock's legacy in *The Merchant of Venice* may symbolize the historical struggle between Jews and Christians over the legacy of the Hebrew Scriptures, a struggle whose traces are recorded in the text as well as in the marginalia of the Bible that Shakespeare read.

Paul metaphorically construes the debate between Christian and Jew in Romans as a will contest between heirs, like the battles for the birthright, 'blessing', or preferment of the father that recur throughout the book of Genesis: 'For the promise that he should be the heir of the world, was not given to Abraham, or to his seed, through the Law but through the righteousness of Faith. For if they which are of the Law be heirs, faith is made void and the promise is made of none effect' (Rom. 4: 13–14). This kind of will contest had been taking place for many generations before Paul, at least according to modern scholars. The Hebrew Bible's twenty-four separate books were all heavily edited products of negotiated compromises among textual claimants expressing opposing viewpoints of Aaronite and Levite priests, the royal houses of David and Saul, the federations of Judah and Israel, and various schools of Prophets.[22] Similar compromises about what would be included in the New Testament were hammered out between Jewish and Hellenized Christians and followers of Peter and followers of Paul. But the central battle in the 1,300-year evolution 'from the corpus to the canon' of what ended up as the Christian Bible, was that between Hebrew and Christian redactors.[23]

Although one school of Gnostic Christians, the Marcionites, regarded the Hebrew Bible as the work of the Devil, most New Testament authors and speakers regarded it as 'Scripture' and alluded to it frequently for the same purposes Jewish authors alluded to earlier texts: 'reinforcing ideological continuity across schools and eras',[24] 'making two stories into one continuous story', and creating 'a sense of absolute historical continuity or recurrence or an assumption that earlier events and figures are timeless ideological models by which all that follows can be measured'.[25] But Paul's project was not to reform

Judaism. Rather it was to use its traditions and dispersed network of congregants as the basis for a new religion not restricted to Israelite inheritance or requiring elaborate ritual observances. Instead Paul appealed to widespread Hellenistic beliefs in dying and resurrected gods and to the cosmopolitanism of the Roman empire of which he was a proud citizen and whose capital was the destination of his most important letter and his final voyage.

This project was best served by subversive and ironic allusion that could 'overwrite' the Hebrew Scriptures and reverse their sense while retaining their expression. For instance, Genesis tells the story of God's selection of Abraham as the founder of a chosen people to rule the geographic area of what came to be called Palestine, a group defined by genetic lineage and marked by circumcision of the organ of generation. Paul rewrites the story to say that Abraham was not selected for breeding purposes, but because he manifested great faith. He equates the very fleshly signifier of a cut penis with a purely symbolic gesture equivalent to any other expression of willingness to give up something for one's faith. And he transforms the word 'Jew' from its ethnic designation to a generic label of faithful: 'For he is not a Jew, which is one outward: neither is that circumcision, which is outward in the flesh. But he is a Jew which is one within, and the circumcision is of the heart, in the spirit, not in the letter, whose praise is not of men, but of God' (Rom. 2: 28–9).

The logical fallacies of such interpretative expropriations are acknowledged, even by Paul's ardent admirers:

The argument... is a sequence of preposterous sophistries.... Paul won the fight against all the odds by a dazzling display of intellectual pyrotechnics, reinforced by his own saintliness and force of character and his converts' loyalty and distaste for the knife. We may be grateful to him for this outrageous logic and for so enabling Christianity to become a world religion; but we should concede that theology deserves a bad name if an acceptable universalism has to be bought at such a price.[26]

Paul's manipulation of allusion in the battle for the legacy of the text displays a tricksterish quality often associated with the character of Jacob. Like Jacob, the second-born son disguising himself as Esau, Paul the follower of Christ masks himself as a traditional Jew to gain the scriptural birthright from an older brother. Paul reconfigures the original story of God's preference of 'Israel'—another name for Jacob and for the Jews—into a story of God's rejection of Israel: 'they are not Israel, which are of Israel. Neither are their children, because they are the seed of Abraham ... they which are the children of the flesh, are not the children of God, but the children of the promise are counted for the seed ... that the purpose of God might remain according to election not by works, but by him that calleth. ... It was said unto [Rebekah], "The elder shall serve the younger [Jacob]." ... I will call them, my people, which were not my people: and her, Beloved, which was not beloved' (Rom. 9: 6–7, 8, 11, 12, 25).

Jacob's trickery is alluded to more than once in *The Merchant of Venice*, first in Shylock's story of the breeding goats and then in the strange scene in which Launcelot switches allegiance from Shylock to Bassanio. After expressing guilt for betraying his old master, Launcelot encounters his blind old father bringing an offering to pass on to his master. Launcelot disguises his identity by letting blind Gobbo feel the back of his head, just as Jacob tricks his father Isaac by using a goatskin to make him feel as hairy as his older brother Esau. Launcelot kneels and says, 'give me your blessing' (2.2.74). At the end of the scene, the father's gift is passed on to the new master, whom Launcelot flatters as more sanctified than his richer predecessor: 'You have the grace of God, sir, and he hath enough' (2.2.145–6).

For Paul, the word 'Jew' remains usefully ambiguous as both honorific and pejorative. The later writers of the gospels make it into a derogatory epithet as well as the designation of a group, and so it remains—as in Launcelot's 'I am a Jew if I serve the Jew any longer' (2.2.107), or Lorenzo's 'she is issue to a faithless Jew' (2.4.37). The gospel writers personify the Jews, represented by Judas, as the enemies of Jesus. The Jews harass and bully him and laugh at his suffering. They scheme relentlessly until they get the Romans to kill him. They attempt to overwrite the story of his resurrection by bribing witnesses into falsifying it. It is the Jews' hatred, portrayed in the gospel stories and perennially revived with later stories of well-poisoning and child murder, which warrants and stimulates Christian hatred against them.[27] Shakespeare follows this order by making Shylock snarl at his first entrance: 'I hate him for he is a Christian ... I will feed fat the ancient grudge I bear him' (1.3.40, 45). And his refusal of the offer of a generous monetary substitution for the forfeited pound of flesh increases his portion of blame. But unlike the Jews in the New Testament, Shakespeare's Shylock is able to make a case for that blame being shared, for the Christians throwing the first stone. 'He hates our sacred nation', he says of Antonio (l. 46), and then to him,

> You call me misbeliever, cut-throat, dog,
> And spit upon my Jewish gaberdine,
>
> .   .   .   .   .
>
> You...void your rheum upon my beard,
> And foot me as you spurn a stranger cur
> Over your threshold.
>
> (1.3.110–17)

Antonio confirms this, 'I am as like to call thee so again, | To spit on thee again, to spurn thee too' (ll. 128–9). In this exchange, 'which is the justice, which is the thief?' (*Lear* 4.5.149–50). Rather than portraying what Lewalski calls 'Christian Love and its antithesis' or what Kermode refers to as 'the supersession in human history of the grim four thousand years of unalleviated justice by the era of love and mercy', Shakespeare may be questioning the validity of such one-sided formulations in their original source.

Paul's project of taking possession of the Hebrew Bible was carried forward a generation or two after he died by the writers of the gospels and the editors who added them and his letters into a new set of Scriptures consisting of the Old and New Testaments. Within this enlarged collection, the repository of Jewish history, law, prophecy, and poetry was transformed into the first section of a tragicomic structure whose downward trajectory was reversed and completed by a revisionary supplement—the 'Good News' of the gospel. New Christians colonized the old book, reducing it to what Harold Bloom has called 'a captive prize'.[28]

The analogous Christian victories of the final act of *The Merchant of Venice* are shadowed. The marriage of Christian and converted Jew is stained by cynicism, the holy retreat claimed by Portia turns out to be a falsification of the truth of her spying on the husband to whom she had given full trust only to discover his betrayal of their pledge, the opening melancholy of Antonio is never relieved, and the music of the spheres so eloquently evoked by Lorenzo is unavailable to those who remain in 'a naughty world' (5.1.91), whether Belmont or Venice.

One explanation for these unresolved cadences is the young comic protagonists' treatment of fathers. Three appear in the course of the play and each is ridiculed or overcome by his junior. Launcelot makes a fool of blind and doddering Gobbo, Jessica deceives and robs cruel and cranky Shylock, and Portia sidesteps 'the will of a dead father' that arbitrarily stipulates that she 'may neither choose who I would nor refuse who I dislike; so is the will of a living daughter curbed' (1.2.22–4). Though comedy, like Pauline Christianity, tends to privilege the young—the twice born, the new man or woman—the claims of the parents, of the old religion and the predecessor text seem to linger. Despite the predictions of the New Testament and the pogroms and expulsions by Christian Europeans, the Jews persisted in retaining the Hebrew Bible and rejecting its Christian revisions. Throughout the Middle Ages Jewish scholars were required to debate with Christians in the hope that their continuing challenge to the faith of the Church could be put to rest by strong scholastic argument.[29] But though the scholars were always declared losers by Christian judges, their perspectives were never eradicated. And though Jew-baiting rivalled bear-baiting as a form of entertainment in the Bankside where stage Jews were held up to opprobrium and ridicule, the presence of Shakespeare's Shylock did as much to tarnish as to burnish the image of the Christian he was meant to foil.

A Masque of Revelation:
The Tempest *as Apocalypse*

I

The Tempest is generally thought to be the last complete play Shakespeare wrote, the final chapter in his book. It certainly is his most mysterious and sublime. Whether or not he intended it as a farewell to his audience, its magician-playwright protagonist prophesies his own death and the dissolution of his world. For those familiar with the Bible, such a strong 'sense of an ending' would suggest the 'Last Things' of its most mysterious final book, The Revelation of St John the Divine, often called the 'Apocalypse'.

The strong influence of the first book of the Bible on *The Tempest*, explored in Chapter 2, does not preclude an equally significant link to the last. Rabbinic authors of the Midrash as well as St Augustine and other patristic commentators held that multiple interpretations of the same text gave evidence of the divine fertility of the original.[1] Genesis relates to Revelation as Alpha to Omega, the first and last letters of the Greek alphabet in which the Apocalypse was written and by which God defines his own totality at its opening and close (Rev. 1: 8; 22: 13). Stanley Wells notes that *The Tempest* is distinguished by 'a structure which looks kaleidoscopically different from every angle...we can follow one strand through the work, but only by shutting our ears and eyes to the others'.[2]

The Tempest was first presented at court on 1 November 1611 as part of the Hallowmas celebrations following Hallowe'en, the day of the dead, one of only two days on which passages from the Apocalypse were read. As a work about endings rather than origins, providence rather than progeny, *The Tempest* enacts a plan long-hatched to correct what has been mistaken, restore what has been usurped, perfect what has been incomplete. This is the story of Revelation, of creation absorbed back into the creator, of a return to Eden where history is concluded. From the vantage point of Revelation, and that of the New Testament in general, everything that happened earlier leads to the conclusion prefigured and premeditated by the Bible's author. Paul says of the events of the Old Testament: 'Now all these things came unto them for examples, and were written to admonish us, upon whom the ends of the world are come' (1 Cor. 10: 11).

As final books in the larger collections they conclude, Revelation and *The Tempest* share a retrospective and epitomizing role in relation to earlier works. The Apocalypse has been called a 'palimpsest' that 'condenses a series of episodes from the history of God's appearance to his people into a single image of this relationship beyond historical time and space'.[3] *The Tempest* takes a similar retrospective stance: it re-stages events occurring before the first scene and it 'reconsiders issues that had occupied Shakespeare's mind from the earliest history plays'.[4]

2

In many of his earlier plays Shakespeare made allusions to the book of Revelation. In *The Tempest* itself, one passage contains an unmistakable quotation of the Apocalypse's strange image of earth swallowing the sea in order to deliver its victims: 'And the serpent cast out of his mouth a flood that he might cause her to be carried away of the flood. But the earth holp the woman and the earth opened her mouth and swallowed up the flood which the dragon had cast out of its mouth' (Rev. 12: 15–16). This is Miranda's plea to her father: 'Had I been any god of power, I would | Have sunk the sea within the earth, or ere | It should the good ship so have swallowed and | The fraughting souls within her' (1.2.10–13).

The words of *The Tempest* identify Prospero with the God of Revelation in language that refers to him, in the powers and behaviour ascribed to him, and in utterances he makes. Miranda most probably means Prospero when she speaks of 'a god of power'; he alludes to

himself as more than merely her father—'I am more better | Than
Prospero...And thy no greater father' (1.2.19–21)—and Ariel
addresses him, 'All hail, great master' (1.2.190). Prospero manifests
the powers of creator and destroyer, punisher and deliverer, that define
the biblical God:

> I have bedimmed
> The noontide sun, called forth the mutinous winds,
> And 'twixt the green sea and the azured vault
> Set roaring war — to the dread rattling thunder
> Have I given fire, and rifted Jove's stout oak
> With his own bolt; the strong-based promontory
> Have I made shake; and by the spurs plucked up
> The pine and cedar...
>
> (5.1.41–8)

Like 'the image of the risen Jesus as keybearer' in Rev. 1: 18 'derived
from Hellenistic conceptions of Hekate', Prospero holds the power to
raise the dead: 'graves at my command | Have waked their sleepers,
oped, and let 'em forth | By my so potent art' (5.1.48–50).[5] Prospero has
hosts of spirit messengers at his command, and, like his human
children and subjects, he addresses them sometimes with 'lovingkind-
ness' and at others with irritation and anger, like the Jesus of Revelation addressing his followers in the seven churches of chs. 2 and 3. And
when the invisible Ariel speaks Prospero's condemnation to the lords
in his control, his language is that of prophets and of Jesus speaking
the words of God (3.3.53–82).

Shakespeare could find precedent for mounting the book of Revelation on stage in the medieval cycles of Corpus Christi plays, which
typically had seven instalments, culminating in a final play called
Antichrist or Judgement, dramatizing the tribulations of the damned,
the punishment of demons often portrayed like clowns, and the debate
before God of the conflicting claims of Justice and Mercy. These
medieval mystery plays also provided a model for representing God
as a human character and actor. He is usually referred to as 'Salvator',
the Saviour, but at the end of the play, like the protagonist of *The
Tempest*, he is acknowledged by the actor playing the role and by the
designation in the script as 'Figura'—as a metaphor rather than a
representation.[6]

3

To readers or viewers expecting a story of events that unfold sequentially within a stable representation of the world, Revelation and *The Tempest* present similar difficulties. Instead of proceeding from beginning to middle to end, events are predicted, enacted, recalled, broken off, and often duplicated. One climactic series of the Apocalypse's plagues is succeeded by two others, the enemies of God are conclusively defeated and yet continually return, the saved are separated from the damned on several occasions. Prospero twice starts and stops the storm, and repeatedly punishes and forgives, removes and replaces his robe, and bids farewell to his art. From their outset both works insist that the end is at hand, that the final hour has come, but the ending of the ending is continually deferred.

With respect to space, settings are otherworldly and discontinuous; one place can turn into another. John moves from the island of Patmos to the court of heaven and from there into spaces that emerge from opening scrolls as meaning from a text. *The Tempest* begins in a storm on board ship then moves to an uninhabited island where the storm appears as an illusion and where different groups of characters have different perceptions of the same landscape. In this universe, the polarity of sameness and difference is superseded by displacement, recurrence, and metamorphosis. As in Dante's *Paradiso*, another final work patterned upon Revelation, 'the poet . . . manages . . . to represent non-representation . . . [in] the form of a "command performance" . . . the whole . . . has no existence, even fictional, beyond the metaphoric . . . paradise and the poem are co-extensive, like the terms of a metaphor . . . there is no reality that is not a sign, pointing to another level of meaning'.[7] Like that of the Apocalypse, 'the unreality of *The Tempest* contributes towards the play's high suggestive power',[8] but that sense of unreality keeps both works from comfortably fitting into any category of narrative. Instead of presenting a story, they are experienced by viewer or reader as a sequence of moving tableaux, animated emblems, text illustrations, or dream visions. Such experiences belong to the genre of masque.

Edgar Allan Poe suggested a connection between masque, Apocalypse, and *The Tempest* when he named the protagonist of his story,

'The Masque of the Red Death', Prince Prospero. Masques are grandiose dramatic spectacles staged for special occasions by aristocracy and royalty in which members of the audience also participate as performers. They eschew realistic representation, translate contemporary political persons, issues, and events into mythological allegory, and make use of music, dance, lighting, and a shifting framework of sets to convey didactic messages. According to Enid Welsford, 'the masque deals . . . with a moment of transformation; it expresses . . . expectancy, crowned by sudden revelation. . . . *The Tempest* like the masque presents a moment of revelation.'[9] The word 'apocalypse' derives from Greek roots signifying the removal of a veil or a mask. Apocalypses claim to reveal the hidden meaning and outcome of history as a vision bestowed by God upon their speakers. The vision is conveyed as a pageant of emblematic spectacles of catastrophe and deliverance performed for the seer, often within the confines of a heavenly court to which he has been magically transported.

Stephen Orgel notes that

Masques were essential to the life of the Renaissance court; their allegories gave a higher meaning to the realities of politics and power, their fictions created heroic roles for the leaders of society . . . appearing in a masque . . . was not merely playing a part . . . a deep truth about the monarchy was . . . embodied in action, and the monarchs were revealed in roles that expressed strongest beliefs about . . . obligations and perquisites of royalty.[10]

Biblical scholars have found a similar link between the masquelike spectacles described in apocalypses and the ritual practices that celebrated and authorized the offices of the Roman imperial court:

The twenty four elders are kings with crowns, and they do obeisance before their king. They acclaim God as king on his throne, present him with golden crowns after the custom of the Roman imperial cult and praise him in the form of an acclamation . . . which probably has its origins in the political arena. The address 'Our Lord and God' may also resonate the acclamation in the imperial cult of Domitian (dominus et deus noster).[11]

In its original setting, the Apocalypse functions to produce and strengthen belief in a divine monarchy. Its literary structure is designed for 'the legitimation of the transcendent authorization of the message . . . for an appeal to transcendent authority is necessitated by either the impossibility or ineffectiveness of an appeal to more rational or mundane structures of thought or authority'.[12]

The final advent of God into his city Jerusalem at the end of the book of Revelation is patterned after such political masques, as was observed by the early Christian theologian Athanasius: 'As when a great king has entered some great city and dwelt in one of the houses in it, such a city is then greatly honoured and no longer does any enemy or bandit come against it ... So also is the case with the king of all.'[13] England's King Richard II encouraged enactments of Revelation's royal advent. During his coronation procession in 1392, a heavenly castle came down out of heaven on ropes, he was welcomed as the bridegroom, and London was envisioned as the bridal chamber and its populace as his betrothed.[14] James I carried on these traditions when he entered London in 1604 and the recorder of the city welcomed him 'with a ... trope drawn from Revelation, inviting him to "come, therefore, O worthiest of Kings as a glorious bridegroome through your Royall chamber"'.[15]

Like King James, Prospero is a ruler who uses masques to express, display, and strengthen his princely power. Prospero's ability to produce effective masques is associated with the power to create wonder —a common objective of politics, art, and religion. Wonder was defined by Renaissance writers and their classical predecessors as 'a systole of the heart'—a unique reaction of soul, mind, and body combining both fear and joy and resulting from an encounter with something uncanny and sublime.[16] Manifestations of God in the Bible are often reported to produce wonder of the sort that makes John 'fall at his feet as though dead' (Rev. 1: 17). 'Miranda', the name of Prospero's daughter, like 'Miracle', the fourteenth-century word for plays about the Bible, signifies wonder. When she is first observed by Ferdinand, he equates wonder with an experience of the divine: 'Most sure the goddess | On whom these airs attend. Vouchsafe my prayer ... O you wonder' (1.2.424–5, 429). When Miranda sees her first young man, she says, 'It carries a brave form. But 'tis a spirit. ... I might call him | A thing divine' (1.2.414, 420–1). Even cynical Sebastian cannot hide his wonder at Prospero's last masque, as he blurts, 'A most high miracle' (5.1.180).

In drama as well as in religious ritual, wonder is promoted by a design principle labelled the 'reveal/conceal dialectic'. The presence of curtains, proscenium arches, and layered backdrops in the indoor theatres for which masques and masquelike plays were written imitates the architecture of cathedrals and temples housing a series of holier and more secret chambers masked by portals, screens, curtains, and cabinets, whereby 'an initiant makes his way through various cultic barriers into the adyton [holy of holies] where the focal religious experience will be staged'.[17] Such nested discovery spaces appear frequently in the book of Revelation, as a door in the heaven opens in 4: 1, the scroll is opened in 6: 1, the temple in heaven is laid open and the ark of the covenant is seen inside it in 11: 19. In *The Tempest*, Prospero has the imprisoned lords taken from a grove of trees surrounding his compound into a charmed circle inside it, where they are released to regard the vision of Ferdinand and Miranda playing chess, which he discovers from behind a curtain (5.1.57sd-73sd[18]).

The use of the theatrical point of view to suggest divine omniscience is similar in apocalypse and masque. The location of the throne of God in the middle of the space of the heavenly vision of Revelation makes him the primary object and the audience of the vision. At masque performances,

the monarch became the centre of the theatrical experience . . . there is only one focal point . . . this is where the king sat and the audience around him at once became a living emblem of the structure of the court . . . the central experience of drama in court then involved not simply the action of a play, but the interaction between the play and the monarch, and the structured organization of the other spectators around him.[19]

Unusual mirroring and framing devices also typify apocalypse and masque. Revelation is itself a vision and it contains visions within it. *The Tempest* is a masque and contains masques. The climactic moment of unmasking, 'when the solution of difficulty, the conquest of adverse powers . . . marked by the sudden appearance of the masquers', transforms the relationship between audience and performers.[20] 'At the end, the stage opened out to include the court, and the noble dancers chose partners from the audience to dance out the revels of earthly and heavenly order in the ultimate theater of the court.'[21] In both Revelation and *The Tempest*, such a transformation occurs twice: first, when the Lamb of God comes down from heaven and takes 'his dwelling among men' in the New Jerusalem (21: 3) and when Prospero comes out of hiding and reveals himself to his countrymen (5.1.161), and second, when, after John's vision has concluded, God speaks directly with the members of John's audience (22: 6–7, 12–16), and when, after all the characters have left the stage, the actor who played Prospero addresses his audience directly in the epilogue in the personae of both the character and its author.

4

In setting out to write a masque with a godlike central character as a concluding work for a large collection of earlier books, it is likely that Shakespeare had Revelation close at hand. Juxtaposing it with *The Tempest* displays systematic parallels of incident and a reciprocal mid-rashic flow of inspiration and interpretation between them. These parallels themselves unmask dark passages, hidden patterns, and obscured rapturous effects.

The book of Revelation and *The Tempest* share a four-part structure consisting of (1) an introduction of setting and participants and movement to another world, (2) a pageant of battles in which good triumphs and evil is defeated, followed by images of resurrection, judgement, and the dissolution of the world, (3) a new pageant combining re-creation with marriage, and (4) the closing of the vision and a return to the setting of this world.

1. John and Miranda are initiates situated on an island. Jesus/God and Prospero are their father-initiators. The first event is a storm. When John is caught up by the Spirit, which appears to him like a roaring wind, he falls 'at his feet as dead' (1: 17). When she first appears, Miranda is horrified by the tempest (1.2.5–13). Each of them is reassured by the father's self-identification: 'Fear not; I am the first and the last' (1: 17), says Jesus. 'Be collected. | No more amazement. Tell your piteous heart | There's no harm done... I am more better... Than ... thy no greater father' (1.2.13–15, 19–21), says Prospero.

John is transported to the divine court, where he sees God sitting on a bejewelled throne that flashes thunder and lightning while four cherubic beasts and twenty-four elders offer tribute and praise (4: 4–11). Prospero puts Miranda to sleep, dons his magic cloak, and is approached by his angelic servant and surrounded by attendants: 'All hail, great master, grave sir, hail.... To answer thy best pleasure... to thy strong bidding task | Ariel and all his quality' (1.2.190–3). In the heavenly court a sealed scroll appears in the hand of God. The Lamb breaks its seal, and, as if they were walking off the page, a series of spectacular tableaux unfolds before the audience of God and his court. Prospero and Ariel move into a space apart from the rest of the characters, visible only to the audience, and here the master devises the scenarios that his minister enacts and reports.

2. In both works the pageant of battles has ten parts. In the first, plagues are loosed. Four horsemen inflict catastrophe upon the inhabitants of the earth below: thunder and lightning, earthquakes and hail, mountains falling into the sea, men making war on one another, 'kings of earth, and the great men and the rich men and the chief captains, and the mighty men, and every bondman and every free man hid themselves in dens and among the rocks of the mountains' (6: 15). Ariel describes the similar plagues he has inflicted earlier at Prospero's behest:

> Jove's lightning, the precursors
> O'th' dreadful thunderclaps
>
> .   .   .   .
>
>   The fire and cracks
> Of sulphurous roaring the most mighty Neptune
> Seem to besiege, and make his bold waves tremble,
> Yea, his dread trident shake.
>
>   (1.2.202–7)

Prospero's enemies experience a sky that seems to 'pour down stinking pitch' (1.2.3), class conflict, howling within 'louder than the weather', prayers of repentance and curses of defiance, and 'a fever of the mad' infecting all their reason (1.2.210). This pageant of disasters brings pleasure to the spectators. In Revelation, 'we give thee thanks ... that thou should give reward unto thy servants' (11: 17–18). In *The Tempest*, Prospero glories, 'My brave spirit. ... Why, that's my spirit!' (1.2.207, 216).

The second part depicts perils and battles from the distant past. In the Bible they appear as what John calls 'portents'. The first two describe a pregnant woman, undergoing a difficult labour and being threatened by a dragon who tries to catch and devour her male child as soon as it is born. God snatches the child up to heaven and protects the fleeing woman with a place prepared for her in the wilderness. Later the frustrated dragon tries to drown the woman with a flood, but she is again saved.[22] This tale resembles that of Miranda's deliverance from flood waters under her father's care. They were left 'To cry to th' sea that roared to us, to sigh | To th'winds' (1.2.149–50), but then were rescued 'By providence divine' (1.2.160). Miranda is a female rather than male child, but, like the threatened babe in the Revelation portent, she too is 'destined to rule all nations', and is for that reason hunted by the tyrant. Prospero adopts the part of the birthing mother: 'When I have decked the sea with drops full salt, | Under my burden groaned; which raised in me | An undergoing stomach, to bear up | Against what should ensue' (1.2.155–8).

The crowned dragon that persecutes parent and child is identified as 'that old serpent, called the devil and Satan, [which] was cast out, which deceiveth all the world' (Rev. 12: 9). The adversary of *The Tempest* who usurped the dukedom, sought to kill parent and child, and leads others astray, is Prospero's brother Antonio. Revelation reports that the dragon and his angels lost the battle with the angel Michael in heaven and were 'thrown down' on to the earth (12: 9), just as Antonio and 'All but mariners | Plunged in the foaming brine and quit the vessel, | Then all afire with [Ariel]' (1.2.211–13). After failing to capture the mother with his flood, the dragon 'went and made war with the remnant of her seed' (12: 17), just as Antonio and 'the men of sin' land on the island and conspire to bring it under their control.

The third part of the battle pageant introduces more monsters. In Revelation, the beast and its offspring, who resemble the dragon and are subject to him, crawl out of the sea, reproduce, 'mouth . . . blasphemy against God' (13: 6), seek wealth and power, conspire against God, and gain considerable influence over the world. In ch. 17, one of the beasts returns, bearing on his back the ugly but alluring witch named 'the Whore of Babylon'—'mother of whoredoms and the abomination of the earth' (17: 5–6). She resembles Prospero's old antagonist, Sycorax, who was banished from Algiers to the island for being a 'damned witch . . . For mischiefs manifold and sorceries terrible | To enter human hearing' (1.2.264–6), who issued 'earthy and abhorred commands' (l. 274), and who mated with the devil to conceive a monstrous son, Caliban (ll. 321–2). After the story of their rescue, Prospero tells Miranda to look upon this 'freckled whelp, hagborn—not honoured with | A human shape' (ll. 284–5) whose ambition, lust, and proclivity for drink are inherited from his mother. In both Revelation and *The Tempest*, good and evil families are symmetrical. The dragon and the beast parody the Father and the Son, just as Sycorax and Caliban parody Prospero and Miranda.

In the fourth part of the battle pageant, the saved appear and are tried. After the beast in Revelation marks his followers with the number 666, the saved enter amid 'the voice of harpers harping with their harps. And they sung as it were a new song' (14: 2–3) and are marked with the name of the Lamb. They are those men 'which are not defiled with women: for they are virgins' (14: 4), contrasted to those with the appetites and lusts of the beast. In *The Tempest*, upon Caliban's exit, Ariel's song, 'Full fathom five thy father lies', accompanies the entrance of Ferdinand, who wonders, 'Where should this music be? I'th' air or th'earth? ... sure it waits upon | Some god o'th' island' (1.2.390–2). He and Miranda are the saved in *The Tempest*; their sexual restraint, once proven, will elicit the father's blessing. The celebration is short-lived. Next, in Revelation, three angels fly in to warn against worship of the beast and threaten dire punishments. Another voice assures the righteous that their torments will be rewarded: 'Blessed are the dead, which hereafter die in the Lord ... for they rest from their labours, and their works follow them' (14: 13). Similarly, Prospero interrupts the blissful meeting, accuses Ferdinand of treason, storms at his daughter, and imposes a test of endurance and restraint upon the lovers, while in asides assuring the audience that he means them well: 'It goes on, I see, | As my soul prompts it. . . . this swift business | I must uneasy make, lest too light winning | Make the prize light' (1.2.422–3, 453–5). At the end of this part, victories are again trumpeted: 'those who had won ... were singing the song of Moses' (Rev. 15: 3) and 'It works. . . . Thou hast done well, fine Ariel' (*Tempest* 1.2.496–7).[23]

The fifth part of the battle pageant elaborates the crimes and the punishments of the evil ones: 'The sanctuary ... was thrown open, and out of it came the seven angels with the seven plagues' (Rev. 15: 2–6); 'Follow me. | Hark what thou else shalt do me' (*Tempest* 1.2.497–8). Like the torments of Dante's *Inferno*, these punishments combine vengeance with warning and symbolic statement by mirroring the sins that brought them on. Just as Revelation's dragon is separated from his offspring the beast for trying to destroy the babe, so Alonso is marooned and deprived of his son in retaliation for exiling Prospero and threatening his daughter.[24] Over-eager Antonio and Sebastian are repeatedly frustrated by the disappearance of their quarry at the moment before capture, and Caliban, Trinculo, and Stefano pay the drunkards' price of falling, with terrible hangovers, into a cesspool. The antagonists of God and Prospero continue to rebel, even in defeat. After the fifth plague, 'They gnawed their tongues for sorrow, and blasphemed the God of heaven for their pains, and for their sores, and repented not of their works' (Rev. 16: 10–11). Similarly, despite the torments of storm, shipwreck, ague, fatigue, hunger, thirst, disorientation, and internal dissension, both sets of *The Tempest*'s conspirators continue to marshal their forces and prepare for a final confrontation. Revelation's God makes the wicked sin: 'For God hath put in their hearts to fulfil his will, and to do with one consent for to give their kingdom unto the beast, until the words of God be fulfilled' (17: 17).[25] By putting Alonso and his counsellor and guardians to sleep, Prospero arranges for Antonio and Sebastian to conspire once again against their rightful ruler (2.1.196–304), and he facilitates the efforts of Caliban, Trinculo, and Stefano to usurp his rule (2.2; 3.2).

The sixth part of the battle pageant elaborates on the Whore of Babylon. 'Drunken with the blood of the saints' (17: 6), after having committed fornication with the kings of the earth, she rides a scarlet monster and bears a large chalice of wine. Stefano comes upon Caliban bearing a wine-bottle he has made out of bark, and sings of his fornication with Moll, Meg, Marian, and Margery (2.2.45–55). Stefano says 'kiss the book', while offering Caliban a drink from his bottle, mocking the Eucharist as well as the royal pageant in which Queen Elizabeth received the English Bible from the allegorical figure of Truth, kissed it, and promised to read therein daily.[26] Caliban responds to Stefano's 'celestial liquor' by worshipping him as a god, mirroring the biblical equation of whoredom, drunkenness, and idolatry.[27] The account of the demise of the Whore of Babylon begins with a description of internal dissension: 'they... shall hate the whore, and shall make her desolate and naked, and shall eat her flesh, and burn her with fire' (17: 16).[28] Prospero arranges for the allied sinners to fall into faction: Antonio and Sebastian cruelly torment Alonso, while Stefano, Trinculo, and Caliban begin cursing one another (3.2.42–87).

The seventh part of the pageant subjects the enemies to judgement and sentencing in the midst of their pleasures. In Revelation, 'another angel came down from heaven, having great power, so that the earth was lightened with his glory' (18: 1). In *The Tempest*, stage directions state: *Thunder and lightning. Ariel ⌈descends⌉, like a harpy, claps his wings upon the table, and . . . the banquet vanishes* (3.3.52). Then the indictment is read. In Revelation, 'It is fallen, it is fallen, Babylon the great city, and is become the habitation of devils, and the hold of all foul spirits, and a cage of every unclean and hateful bird . . . and the kings of the earth have committed fornication with her, and the merchants of the earth are waxed rich of the abundance of her pleasures' (18: 2–3). In *The Tempest*,

> You are three men of sin, whom destiny—
> That hath to instrument this lower world
> And what is in't—the never-surfeited sea
> Hath caused to belch up you,
>
> .   .   .   .   .
>
> Being most unfit to live.
>
> (3.3.53–6, 58)

Next, the sentence is pronounced. In Revelation, 'In the cup that she hath filled to you, fill her double. Therefore shall her plague come at one day, death, sorrow, and famine, and she shall be burnt with fire' (18: 6, 8). In *The Tempest*,

> I have made you mad,
>
> .   .   .   .   .
>
> The powers, delaying not forgetting, have
> Incensed the seas and shores . . .
>   Thee of thy son, Alonso,
> They have bereft, and do pronounce by me
> Ling'ring perdition
>
> (3.3.58, 73–7)

This is accompanied by a reprieve offered to any who will repent. In Revelation, 'Go out of her my people, that ye be not partakers in her sins, and that ye receive not of her plagues' (18: 4). In *The Tempest*, 'whose wraths to guard you from . . . is nothing but heart's sorrow | And a clear life ensuing' (3.3.79, 81–2). Finally, the grief of the punished is displayed. In Revelation, 'the kings of the earth shall bewail... saying, Alas, alas the great city.... the merchants of the earth shall weep and wail.... And every shipmaster and all the people that occupy ships ... shall cast dust on their heads' (18: 9, 10, 11, 17). In *The Tempest* Alonso moans,

> O, it is monstrous, monstrous!
> Methought the billows spoke and told me of it,
> The winds did sing it to me,
>
> .   .   .   .   .
>
> Therefor my son i'th' ooze is bedded, and
> I'll seek him deeper than e'er plummet sounded,
> And with him there lie mudded.
>   (3.3.95–7, 100–2)

The eighth part of the battle pageant shifts to a wedding feast of the saved. After yet another throne-room victory vaunt—Revelation's 'Hallelujah, salvation and glory, and honour, and power be to the Lord our God' (19: 1), and *The Tempest's* 'My high charms work, | And these mine enemies... now are in my power' (3.3.88–90)—the heavenly chorus anticipates marriage: 'Let us be glad and rejoice... for the marriage of the Lamb is come, and his wife hath made herself ready.... Blessed are they which are called unto the Lamb's supper' (19: 7–9). Prospero does the same: 'In these fits I leave them, while I visit | Young Ferdinand... and his and mine loved darling' (3.3.91–3). He congratulates them for passing his tests and in the form of an extended masque (4.1.59–138) presents them with a vision of the greater joys they are promised.

During the ninth part the celebration is interrupted and the battles are concluded. In the heavenly court the wedding festivity is shattered by a new portent: 'I saw heaven open, and behold a white horse, and he that sat upon him was called, Faithful and True.... And the warriors which were in heaven followed him upon white horses...' (19: 11, 14). The masque in Prospero's court is broken off by a resumption of the hostilities with the rebels (4.1.143), and Ariel is dispatched to lead the battle—'Spirit, | We must prepare to meet with Caliban. | Ay, my commander' (4.1.165–7). Jesus' forces defeat the armies of the beast and the false prophet, who are 'cast into a lake of fire, burning with brimstone' (19: 20), while Stefano, Trinculo, and Caliban, whom

Prospero again calls 'A devil, a born devil' (4.1.188), are thrown into a 'filthy-mantled pool...dancing up to th' chins, that the foul lake | O'er-stunk their feet' (4.1.182–4).

The tenth part concludes this pageant with confinement, release, and judgement. In Revelation, the dragon is chained up in an abyss for a thousand years (20: 1–3). In *The Tempest* Antonio and the men of sin are 'Confined...prisoners, sir, | In the lime-grove...They cannot budge till your release' (5.1.7–11). In Revelation, the dead are awakened and quickly sentenced:

And I saw the dead, both great and small, stand before God: and the books were opened, and another book was opened, which is the book of life, and the dead were judged of those things, which were written in the books, according to their works. And whosoever was not found written in the book of life, was cast into the lake of fire. (20: 12, 15).

The Tempest's action follows suit. At Prospero's behest, 'the mariners asleep | Under the hatches' (5.1.100–1) are brought before him amazed to have returned to life: 'We were dead of sleep...We were awaked; straightway at liberty; | Where we in all her trim freshly beheld | Our royal, good, and gallant ship' (5.1.233, 238–40).

Alonso and the royals who were confined in madness and catatonia are placed in a charmed circle Prospero has drawn in front of his seat, and, as they gradually come to, they are judged on the basis of their deeds. First Gonzalo, like the martyrs who 'reigned with Christ' because they 'did not worship the beast' (20: 4), is promised his reward: 'O good Gonzalo, | My true preserver, and a loyal sir | To him thou follow'st, I will pay thy graces | Home both in word and deed' (5.1.68–71).

Next Alonso is reprimanded for cruelty in exiling the Duke. Then Sebastian is sentenced to tormenting pinches for complicity in the plot (5.1.74). Finally Antonio, 'brother mine, that entertained ambition, | Expelled remorse and nature, [who] Would here have killed your king' (5.1.75–6, 78), is condemned to 'inward pinches...most strong' (l. 77).

3. The end of the judgement sequences in Revelation and *The Tempest* marks a major structural division in both works. At this moment, all that precedes is to be superseded, all that has remained hidden is to be disclosed, all that has been promised and deferred is to

be fulfilled. In the first verse of ch. 21, the current framework of John's vision dissolves. Ever since the door of heaven opened in ch. 4 and he was transported upwards by the Spirit, he has resided in the heavenly court, looking out at the masquelike visions presented before him and down at the earth below as it is blasted by wars and natural disasters. But now, both heaven and earth vanish, along with the sea. 'Behold I make all things new' (21: 4) calls a voice from the throne. A similar dissolution of heaven and earth is envisioned by Prospero in his speech at the end of the wedding masque:

> Our revels now are ended. These our actors,
> As I foretold you, were all spirits, and
> Are melted into air, into thin air;
> And like the baseless fabric of this vision,
> The cloud-capped towers, the gorgeous palaces,
> The solemn temples, the great globe itself,
>   ... shall dissolve;
> And, like this insubstantial pageant faded,
> Leave not a rack behind.
>
>   (4.1.148–56)

The dissolution of heaven and earth makes way for a new order, which is also a restoration. The God who withdrew to heaven after his dispute with Adam and Eve now 'will dwell with them: and they shall be his people, and God himself shall be their God with them' (21: 3). The one on the throne who throughout Revelation has spoken only through the intermediaries of Christ and the angels now speaks for himself: 'Behold, I make all things new... I am the beginning and the end' (21: 5–6). Prospero creates a new reality with similar gestures of self-disclosure and intimacy. After abjuring his rough magic, breaking his staff, and drowning his book, he removes the sorcerer's cloak and puts on his hat and rapier in order to 'myself present | As I was sometime Milan' (5.1.85–6). As they emerge from the captivity of their fits, he displays his true self to those who have hitherto experienced his presence only in miraculous acts of punishment and deliverance or through the prophetic voice of his angel: 'Behold, sir King, | The wrongèd Duke of Milan, Prospero.... howsoe'er you have | Been jostled from your senses, know for certain | That I am Prospero' (5.1.108–9, 159–61). Here he follows 'the "I am" self-disclosure formula' conventional in Graeco-Roman as well as Hebrew and Christian apocalypses.[29] God is the sovereign over the kings of the earth and his people (21: 22) previously under the yoke of the beast. Prospero 'requires' his dukedom back from his brother.

The once and future principalities are manifested in yet another pageant, which concludes with displays of reconciliation between opposites: power and love, garden and city, Naples and Milan. In Revelation, the pageant's presenter is an angel who had earlier delivered one of the plagues. 'Come, I will show thee the bride, the Lamb's wife' (21: 9), he says to John, and he takes him to 'a great and high mountain' (21: 10) to watch the holy city of Jerusalem coming down out of heaven from God. 'I will requite you with . . . a wonder to content ye' (5.1.171–2), says Prospero as he conducts the lords to the threshold of his cell and there *discovers Ferdinand and Miranda playing at chess* (5.1.171sd). Alonso refers to this *tableau vivant* as 'A vision of the island' (5.1.178), Sebastian as 'a most high miracle' (5.1.180). Both visions are exalted representations of political marriage that brings peace on earth. In the New Jerusalem, 'the leaves of the tree served to heal the nations' (22: 2) rent apart since Babel, and the nations walk freely through its open gates (21: 25). In the New Italy, where the bride will 'be' Milan and the groom will 'be' Naples, two rival city-states will achieve a union symbolized by Miranda and Ferdinand's love-play over the game-board.

In addition to its political statement, the concluding conjugal vision of these two divine comedies has theological dimensions stemming from the traditional interpretation of the Hebrew Bible's Song of Songs, whose erotic lyrics were ascribed to the love of God. The sanctified marriage between the bride of Jerusalem and the Lamb contrasts with the illicit union between the Whore of Babylon and the beast. Though Ferdinand and Miranda burn with ardour, Cupid and Venus are still banned from their entertainments (4.1.84–101), and Prospero has come to trust that, when he opens the curtain, the lovers will be observed in honourable play rather than doing what Caliban or Stefano would in 'murkiest den' or 'opportune place' (4.1.25–6). Though Jerusalem's gates are never shut, 'there shall enter into it none unclean thing' (21: 27). Like the infinitely prosperous winterless world of springtime and harvest that the father conjured up for the bride and groom in *The Tempest*'s wedding masque, Revelation's bride city is also an edenic garden where trees of life growing on the banks of a river yield a different crop every month.

As Prospero's final vision of the lovers is regarded in silent rapture by the lords, Ferdinand and Miranda become aware that they are being watched and watch back with the same wonder they inspire (5.1.181–7). But this zenith of wonder, when all regard one another as divine spirits or as performers on a stage, soon passes. The lords and the lovers begin to experience each other as real. This is the masque's climactic moment—a moment, says Stephen Orgel, that 'was nearly always the same: the fiction opened outward to include the whole court, as masquers descended from pageant car or stage and took partners from the audience. What the noble spectator watched he ultimately became.'[30]

4. At the conclusion of Revelation and *The Tempest*, the 'opening outward' from Patmos and Prospero's island dissolves barriers between seer and reader, performer and audience, vision time and 'real' time. Once the New Jerusalem is reached by John, it immediately fades, and he never returns to the heavenly court. At the vision's climax God had addressed him directly from within the heavenly city: 'And he said unto me, "Write: for these words are faithful and true"' (21: 6). In the last chapter, the same words are repeated as a memory of an experience already past and a prediction of one to come: 'And he said unto me, "These words are faithful and true . . . Behold, I come shortly"' (22: 6–7). John reassembles his identity as a person in time and space: 'And I am John which heard and saw these things' (22: 8). The angel at whose feet he falls lifts him up saying, 'See thou do it not: for I am thy fellow servant, and of thy brethren the Prophets, and of them which keep the words of this book: worship God' (22: 9). Having completed his passage through a series of trials and revelations, he is now invited to participate in a communion that extends to readers of his book.

Similarly, after the royal party has passed from being one another's visions into one another's reality, Prospero urges Alonso to get up from his knees in a tone of humility expressing his own recently transformed awareness that, like the angel, he speaks not with the voice of God addressing a novitiate but rather with that of a brother and fellow communicant: 'There, sir, stop. | Let us not burden our remembrance with | A heaviness that's gone' (5.1.201–3). As secular time resumes, the vision already past is recollected, reflected upon, and written down so that it can be preserved: God says, 'Seal not the words of the prophecy of this book . . .' (22: 10). Gonzalo insists that they 'set . . . down | With gold on lasting pillars' (5.1.210–11) a record of this occasion of revelation and self-discovery to which 'you gods . . . have chalked forth the way' (5.1.204–6) when 'in one voyage . . . all of us ourselves [did find] | When no man was his own' (5.1.211, 215–16).

The masque's transition from presentation to participation is completed in the epilogues of both works. In Revelation, the union of God and human, speaker and hearer, is expressed with a series of invitations that echo the conjugal exchanges from the Song of Songs and recall the visionary wedding pageants, but now are uttered on the old earth and directed to John's audience: 'And the Spirit and the bride say, "Come." And let him that heareth, say, "Come": and let whosoever will, take of the water of life freely . . . Surely, I come quickly' (22: 17, 20).

With half a turn to the audience in the Banqueting House when the play was performed at court, Prospero says, 'Sir, I invite your highness and your train | To my poor cell, where you shall take your rest | For this one night' (5.1.304–6). The first words of his last speech as Duke of Milan, 'I'll deliver all' (5.1.317), retain the diction of a former God of Power. But they refer specifically to details of 'the story of . . . [his] life' (l. 316) that have not yet been told, and to the 'calm seas, auspicious gales' (l. 318) that will carry the King's fleet home. Prospero's final utterance is 'Please you, draw near' (5.1.323). 'You' here again refers not only to the stage lords, but also to the audience. 'Exeunt' directs the characters to disappear. And yet the speaker of the epilogue remains present, no longer representing only Prospero but the actor who plays him and the creator who made him, addressing people with whom a theatrical revelation has been shared. He implores them to 'release me . . . With the help of your good hands. | Gentle breath of yours my sails | Must fill, or else my project fails, | Which was to please' (Epilogue 9–13). As they 'deliver' applause and cheers, spectators become participants in the fiction while theatrical character becomes actor or author.

In Revelation, the request for involvement also produces a response. A new voice is briefly but unmistakably heard—the voice of the bride just mentioned—which is also the voice of the congregation accepting the invitation with an invitation of its own: 'Amen. Even so come, Lord Jesus' (22: 20). After the noise in Shakespeare's theatre died down, Prospero may have gestured in such a way that the audience, their hands still tingling, would have brought and held their palms together as he concluded:

> Now I want
> Spirits to enforce, art to enchant;
> And my ending is despair
> Unless I be relieved by prayer,
> Which pierces so, that it assaults
> Mercy itself, and frees all faults.
> As you from crimes would pardoned be,
> Let your indulgence set me free.
>
> (Epilogue 14–20)

If that were the case, his last lines of benediction would have echoed the last line of the Bible as well: 'The grace of our Lord Jesus Christ be with you all. Amen' (22: 21).

5

Similarities between *The Tempest* and the book of Revelation illuminate both texts, but so do their differences. Three stand out at the end. Unlike God, who fully realizes his omnipotence, casts out his enemies, and seals up history, Prospero renounces divinity, forgives those who wronged him, and leaves the final outcome of events open. These discrepancies may signify an intention to critique the ideology of divine-right monarchy maintained by King James and other seventeenth-century European rulers.[31] Some have surmised that they express Shakespeare's repudiation of the biblical idea of an end to history 'in an age too late for apocalypse, too critical for prophecy';[32] that Shakespeare sought to 'demystify the apocalypse and thereby humanize it... to turn responsibility for the shaping of history over to man and thereby secularize the Christian prophecy';[33] that he was translating the biblical story about underlying metaphysical reality into an early-modern story about theatrical illusion 'in an age when Apocalypse was in the air, while the traditional images of it were being recognized as mere images'.[34]

But it also may signify that in his conclusion Shakespeare preferred to revert to the model of Joseph at the end of Genesis or to an identification between Prospero and the Jesus of the gospels whose 'kenosis' or relinquishment of divinity to suffer as a mortal for the sake of his subjects provided a different paradigm for the glorification of rulers. Jesus' willingness to forgive his tormenters expressed in the words from the Lord's Prayer echoed in Prospero's last words was also a model for the administration of royal pardons.

The book of Revelation concludes with its author's assertion of finality.

For I protest unto every man that heareth the words of the prophecy of this book, if any man shall add unto these things, God shall add unto him the plagues, that are written in the book. And if any man shall diminish of the words of this book of this prophecy, God shall take away his part out of the Book of life, and out of the holy city, and for those things which are written in this book. (22: 18–19)

These words insist on the completeness of the book and therefore of the Bible as a whole. They claim an eternal stability of the text as it stands, pre-empting both prior claims and future revisions. *The Tempest*, by contrast, is not the last piece of writing that Shakespeare produced—he collaborated in three later plays—and some have been struck by its inconclusiveness rather than its finality: 'The sense of unfinished business is finally the life of the play. Prospero's is a story for which Shakespeare provides no ending.'[35]

But though *The Tempest* concludes open-endedly with a human creator's acknowledgement of fallibility, limitation, and mortality, it has been resurrected by its admiring readers and critical redactors into a complete and perennial corpus, along with the big book in which it was placed as a capstone. Those who assembled the canon of the First Folio, Shakespeare's friends and his colleagues in the King's Men, insisted that it was 'published according to the true originall copies'.[36] They also insisted, like Protestant biblical commentators, that the text was the source of its own vindication:

Read him therefore; and again and again: And if then you do not like him, surely you are in some manifest danger not to understand him. And so we leave you to other of his friends, whom if you need can be your guides: if you need them not you can lead your selves, and others. And such readers we wish him.[37]

They countered his acceptance of mortality with apotheosis: 'Thou art alive still while thy book doth live | And we have wits to read and praise to give ... Stay I see thee in the Hemisphere | Advanced and made a constellation there.'[38] And they refuted Prospero's admission that the theatre was ephemeral by envisioning an encore in which his author's book of plays itself becomes his Second Coming:

> From the world's stage to the grave's tiring room.
> We thought thee dead, but this thy printed worth
> Tells the spectators that thou wentst but forth
> To enter with applause. An actor's art
> Can die and live, to act a second part
> That's but an exit of mortality
> This a re-entrance to a plaudite.[39]

Notes

CHAPTER I

1. *North to Lake Superior: The Journal of Charles W. Penny, 1840*, ed. James L. Carter and Ernest H. Rankin (Marquette, Mich.: The John M. Longyear Research Library, 1970), 34.
2. *Marx and Engels on Literature and Art: A Selection*, ed. Lee Baxandall and Stefan Morowski (St Louis/Milwaukee: Telos Press, 1973), 147.
3. A good deal of ink has been spilled over fruitless conjectures that Shakespeare's name is embedded in the King James translation of Psalm 46. See e.g. *American Notes and Queries* (Oct 1977), 21.
4. See Peter Blayney, *The Shakespeare First Folio* (Washington: Folger Publications, 1991), 25–9, for discussion of Folio prices, and *Book Auction Records* (Folkestone, Pa.: Wm. Dawson, 1996), and *American Book Prices Current* (New York: Bancroft-Parkman, 1996), for King James Bible prices.
5. *The Holy Bible*, A V, Dedication, para. 3.
6. Ben Jonson, 'To the memory of my beloved . . .', in *William Shakespeare: The Complete Works*, ed. Stanley Wells and Gary Taylor (Oxford: Clarendon Press, 1994), p. xlv.
7. This is not to discount the importance of many interpretative studies of individual plays and the Bible published in critical essays or in parts of books, to which my indebtedness is acknowledged throughout. Three short overviews are found in Roy Battenhouse, 'Shakespeare and the Bible', *The Gordon Review*, 8 (1964), 18–24; Peter Milward, SJ, *Shakespeare's Religious Background* (Bloomington, Ind.: Indiana University Press (1973), 85–103; and James Black, *'Edified by the Margent': Shakespeare and the Bible* (Calgary: Faculty of Humanities, University of Calgary, 1979).
8. See 'Preface' to *Poems* (1815), in *Literary Criticism of William Wordsworth*, ed. Paul M. Zall (Lincoln, Nebr.: University of Nebraska Press, 1966), 150–1.
9. Naseeb Shaheen, *Biblical References in Shakespeare's Comedies* (Newark, Del.: University of Delaware Press, 1993); *Biblical References in Shakespeare's History Plays* (Newark, Del.: University of Delaware Press, 1989); *Biblical References in Shakespeare's Tragedies* (Newark, Del.: University of Delaware Press, 1987). These volumes expand and revise the earlier work of Richmond Noble, *Shakespeare's Biblical Knowledge* (London: SPCK, 1935; repr. 1969). Peter Milward, *Biblical Influences in Shakespeare's Great Tragedies*

(Bloomington, Ind.: Indiana University Press, 1987), is also devoted to elucidating specific references and echoes.

10. Robert Alter, *The Art of Biblical Narrative* (New York: Basic Books, 1981); *The Art of Biblical Poetry* (New York: Basic Books, 1985); *The Literary Guide to the Bible* [with Kermode] (Cambridge, Mass.: Harvard University Press, 1987); *The Pleasures of Reading* (New York: Simon & Schuster, 1989); *The World of Biblical Literature* (New York: Basic Books, 1992). Harold Bloom, *Ruin the Sacred Truths: Poetry and Belief from the Bible to the Present* (Cambridge, Mass.: Harvard University Press, 1989); *The Book of J* (New York: Grove Weidenfeld, 1990). Northrop Frye: *The Great Code: The Bible and Literature* (New York: Harcourt Brace Jovanovich, 1982); *Words with Power: Being a Second Study of 'The Bible and Literature'* (San Diego: Harcourt Brace Jovanovich, 1990). Frank Kermode, *The Sense of an Ending* (London: Oxford University Press, 1967); *The Genesis of Secrecy: On the Interpretation of Narrative* (Cambridge, Mass.: Harvard University Press, 1979).

11. Alter, *The World of Biblical Literature*, 20.

12. Frye, *The Great Code*, 12.

13. T. W. Baldwin, *William Shakespere's small Latine & lesse Greeke* (Urbana, Ill.: University of Illinois Press, 1944), 685 ff.

14. Naseeb Shaheen, 'Shakespeare's Knowledge of the Bible—How Acquired', *Shakespeare Studies*, 20 (1988), 206.

15. Gail Paster, 'The Idea of London in Masque and Pageant', in David Bergeron (ed.), *Pageantry in the Shakespearian Theatre* (Athens, Ga.: University of Georgia Press, 1985), 66.

16. James I, *Basilikon Doron 1599* (Menston: The Scolar Press, 1969).

17. Cited by Graham Parry, *The Seventeenth Century: The Intellectual and Cultural Context of English Literature, 1603–1700* (London: Longman, 1989), 23.

18. Ibid. 17.

19. James I, *Basilikon Doron*, 121.

20. Parry, *The Seventeenth Century*, 18.

21. Peter S. Donaldson, *Machiavelli and the Mystery of State* (Cambridge, Mass.: Harvard University Press, 1988), 31.

22. Cited by Jonathan Goldberg, *James I and the Politics of Literature* (Baltimore: Johns Hopkins University Press, 1983), 68.

23. John Donne, 'Expostulation 19', in Sister Elizabeth Savage, SSJ (ed.), *Devotions Upon Emergent Occasions*, Salzburg Studies in English Literature, 21 (Salzburg: Institut für Englische Sprache und Literatur, Universität Salzburg, 1975), ii. 139–40; repr. in M. H. Abrams *et al.*, *The Norton Anthology of English Literature*, 6th edn. (New York: W. W. Norton, 1993), 1124.

24. Sir Philip Sidney, 'A Defence of Poetry', in *Miscellaneous Prose of Sir Philip Sidney*, ed. Katherine Duncan-Jones and Jan van Dorsten (Oxford: Clarendon Press, 1973), 80.

25. For samples, see the monthly letters column in *Bible Review (BR)*.

26. Alvin Kernan, *Shakespeare, the King's Playwright* (New Haven: Yale University Press, 1995), xxi.

27. Arthur Kinney, 'Shakespeare's *Comedy of Errors* and the Nature of Kinds', *Studies in Philology*, 85/1 (Winter 1988), 33. See also Patricia Parker, 'Shakespeare and the Bible: *The Comedy of Errors*', *Recherches semiotiques/ Semiotic Inquiry*, 13 (1993), 67.

28. G. Wilson Knight, *Principles of Shakespearian Production* (New York: Macmillan, 1937), 34.

29. A. C. Bradley, *Shakespearian Tragedy* (London: Macmillan, 1937; repr. of 1905 edn.), 25.

30. R. M. Frye, *Shakespeare and Christian Doctrine* (Princeton: Princeton University Press, 1963), 7.

31. Debra Shuger, *The Renaissance Bible: Scholarship, Sacrifice, and Subjectivity* (Berkeley: University of California Press, 1994), 5.

32. Alter, *The World of Biblical Literature*, 40–5.

33. V. A. Kolve, *The Play Called Corpus Christi* (Stanford, Calif.: Stanford University Press, 1966), 31.

34. C. H. McIlwain, *Political Works of James I* (Cambridge, Mass.: Harvard University Press, 1918), 307.

35. *The Poems of Sir Walter Ralegh*, ed. Agnes Latham (Cambridge, Mass.: Harvard University Press, 1962), 51.

36. Jane Smiley, *A Thousand Acres* (New York: Knopf, 1992).

37. Alter, *The Pleasures of Reading*, 116.

38. Alter, *The World of Biblical Literature*, 85.

39. For use of CE and BCE see General Note at the beginning of the book.

40. Joseph Heineman, 'The Nature of the Aggadah', in Geoffrey H. Hartman and Sanford Budick (eds.), *Midrash and Literature* (New Haven: Yale University Press, 1986), 45.

41. *The Encyclopedia of the Jewish Religion* (New York: Holt, Rinehart, & Winston, 1966), 262. For examples of traditional midrash, see Samuel Rapaport, *Tales and Maxims from the Midrash* (New York: Benjamin Blom, 1971). Modern examples include Frederick Buechner, *Son of Laughter* (San Francisco: Harper, 1993); the essay collection by Alicia Ostriker, *The Nakedness of the Fathers: Biblical Visions and Revisions* (New Brunswick, NJ: Rutgers University Press, 1994); and the critical study by Leslie Brisman, *The Voice of Jacob: On the Composition of Genesis* (Bloomington, Ind.: Indiana University Press, 1990).

42. *The Jewish Encyclopedia* (New York: Ktav, 1964), viii. 548.
43. Harold Fisch, 'The Hermeneutic Quest in *Robinson Crusoe*', in Hartman and Budick (eds.), *Midrash and Literature*, 230.
44. David Stern, *Midrash and Theory: Ancient Jewish Exegesis and Contemporary Literary Studies* (Evanston, Ill.: Northwestern University Press, 1996), 1.
45. Fisch, 'The Hermeneutic Quest', 230.
46. Stern, *Midrash and Theory*, 3. As mentioned earlier, Shakespeare died seven years before the publication of the Folio edition of his plays and there is no evidence that he was involved in either its ordering or its editing. However, it is possible that he had some ideas about publishing his plays as a book, since his contemporary fellow playwright Ben Jonson published a Folio version of his own works. The Bible itself, although referred to as 'The Book', 'The Good Book', etc., developed as a collection of many books, assembled and redacted by later editors into the form of a single volume.
47. Several plays not discussed here have been profitably compared with books or extended passages in the Bible. *The Comedy of Errors* is linked through setting and themes to Paul's letter to the Ephesians by Kinney and Parker. Russell Fraser explores biblical connections to *As You Like It* in 'Shakespeare's Book of Genesis', *Comparative Drama*, 25/2 (Summer 1991), 121–9. Chris Hassell Jr. makes illuminating comparisons in 'Last Words and Last Things: St. John, Apocalypse, and Eschatology in *Richard III*', *Shakespeare Studies*, 18 (1986), 25–40.
48. Alter, *The Pleasures of Reading*, 133–40.

CHAPTER 2

1. Northrop Frye, *The Great Code: The Bible and Literature* (New York: Harcourt Brace Jovanovich, 1982), 106–14.
2. *OED* def. 4, from Latin *tempestas*.
3. Northrop Frye, *Words With Power: Being a Second Study of 'The Bible and Literature'* (San Diego, Calif.: Harcourt Brace Jovanovich, 1990), 40.
4. J. P. Fokkelmann, 'Genesis', in Robert Alter and Frank Kermode (eds.), *The Literary Guide to the Bible* (Cambridge, Mass.: Harvard University Press, 1987), 41.
5. See Steven Marx, 'Progeny: *Prospero's Books*, Genesis and *The Tempest*', *Renaissance Forum*, 2.1, at <http://www.hull.ac.uk/Hull/EL_Web/renforum/v1no2/marx.htm>.
6. To my knowledge, Roy Battenhouse in 'Shakespeare and the Bible', *Gordon Review*, 8 (1964), 20, is the only critic to remark upon these parallels.

7. J. P. Fokkelmann, 'Genesis', 54.
8. *The Tempest*, ed. Stephen Orgel (Oxford: Oxford University Press, 1987), 55.

CHAPTER 3

1. See Richard Elliott Friedman, *Who Wrote the Bible?* (New York: Harper, 1989).
2. Patrick Miller, *The Divine Warrior in Early Israel* (Cambridge, Mass.: Harvard University Press, 1973), 154.
3. Steven Marx, 'Moses and Machiavellism', *Journal of the American Academy of Religion*, 65/3 (Autumn 1997), 551–71.
4. *The Prince*, trans. Peter Bondanella and Mark Musa (Oxford: Oxford University Press, 1984), 55.
5. *The Discourses of Niccolò Machiavelli*, trans. Leslie J. Walker (London: Routledge & Paul, 1975), 547.
6. Ibid. 235.
7. *The Prince*, 58–9.
8. *The Discourses of Niccolò Machiavelli*, 237.
9. 'It was owing to wise men having taken note of this that belief in miracles arose and that miracles are held in high esteem even by religions that are false; for to whatever they owed their origin, sensible men made much of them and their authority caused everybody to believe in them', ibid. 244.
10. Peter S. Donaldson, *Machiavelli and the Mystery of State* (Cambridge: Cambridge University Press, 1988), 172.
11. See e.g. Erik H. Erikson, *Young Man Luther* (New York: Norton, 1958).
12. David Evett, 'Types of King David in Shakespeare's Lancastrian Tetralogy', *Shakespeare Studies*, 14 (1981), 139.
13. *The Prince*, 21.
14. Donaldson, *Machiavelli and the Mystery of State*, 215–16.

CHAPTER 4

1. Jan Kott, *Shakespeare Our Contemporary* (New York: Doubleday Anchor, 1966), 154.
2. 'On Sitting Down to Read King Lear Once Again', in *Poetical Works of John Keats*, ed. H. W. Garrod (Oxford: Clarendon Press, 1939), 482.
3. *The Book of Job* (San Francisco: North Point Press, 1987), p. vii.
4. S. T. Coleridge, *Table Talk*, 29 December 1822, cited in *King Lear*, ed. Kenneth Muir (London: Methuen, 1972), p. xlvii.
5. *Ruin the Sacred Truths* (Cambridge, Mass.: Harvard University Press, 1989), 19.

6. The term 'Old Testament' is used here to refer to the version of the Hebrew Bible included within the Christian Bible, rather than the Masoretic text of the Hebrew Bible used by Jews, which places the literary books or 'Writings' in a later location.

7. Cited by Marvin Pope in *Anchor Bible: Job* (New York: Doubleday, 1973), pp. xxx–xxxi.

8. 'A Defence of Poetry', *Miscellaneous Prose of Sir Philip Sidney*, ed. Katherine Duncan-Jones and Jan van Dorsten (Oxford: Clarendon Press, 1973), 80.

9. l. 1647, cited by William Elton, *King Lear and the Gods* (San Marino, Calif.: The Huntington Library, 1966), 64.

10. Aeschylus, *The Oresteia*, trans. Robert Fagles (New York: Bantam, 1975), ll. 177–9, 182.

11. Citations of *King Lear* are to the Folio text unless marked by (Q) indicating Quarto text.

12. *Aristotle's Poetics*, trans. Leon Golden (Englewood Cliffs, NJ.: Prentice-Hall, 1968), 13, 14.

13. Ibid. 19–20.

14. 'Recognition ... is a change from ignorance to knowledge, bringing about either a state of friendship or one of hostility on the part of those who have been marked out for good fortune or bad', ibid. 19.

15. Ibid.

16. See Robert Pack, 'Betrayal and Nothingness: The Book of Job and *King Lear*', *The Long View* (Amherst, Mass.: University of Massachusetts Press, 1991), 251–76.

17. *Aristotle's Poetics*, 11.

18. Alicia Ostriker, *The Nakedness of the Fathers* (New Brunswick, NJ.: Rutgers University Press, 1994), 234.

19. Richard B. Sewall, *The Vision of Tragedy* (New Haven: Yale University Press, 1980), 4–5.

20. *Aristotle's Poetics*, 12.

21. See Jack Miles, *God: A Biography* (New York: Random House, 1996), 308–28.

22. Moshe Greenberg, 'Job' in Robert Alter and Frank Kermode, *The Literary Guide to the Bible* (Cambridge, Mass.: Harvard University Press, 1987), 301.

23. Jan Kott, *Shakespeare Our Contemporary*, 158.

24. Cited by William Elton, *King Lear and the Gods*, 30–1.

25. See C. G. Jung, *Answer to Job* (Princeton, NJ.: Princeton University Press, 1969), 16–24, and Miles, *God: A Biography*, 325: 'Morally...Job has won. The Lord has lost. God atones for his wrongdoing by doubling Job's initial fortune.'

26. A. C. Bradley, *Shakespearean Tragedy* (New York: Macmillan, 1905), 228.

27. Paul Siegel, *Shakespearean Tragedy and the Elizabethan Compromise* (New York: New York University Press, 1957), 185–6.

28. Marvin Pope, *Anchor Bible: Job*, p. xxiv. Both endings, however, can support an orthodox reading. In the first ending, God responds directly to Job's complaints and questions. His long speech about the beauty and terror of nature leaves the reader who 'hears' it in the dark, but makes complete sense to Job who in 'seeing' God with his own eyes gets beyond the need for explanation: 'I have heard of thee by the hearing of the ear, but now mine eye seeth thee' (42: 5). In the second prose ending, which scholars refer to as 'folktale' or 'epilogue', God vindicates Job for speaking the truth, appoints him to serve as a protector of the comforters, and restores his wealth and family. But Job is given no reason why he suffered, while the reader is privy to the explanation involving God's initial wager with Satan.

29. Kenneth Muir, *King Lear: Critical Essays* (New York: Garland, 1984), 289–90.

CHAPTER 5

1. Reported in Matt. 7: 1–2, Luke 6: 37, Mark 4: 24, Rom. 2: 1, 1 Cor. 4: 3.

2. Roy Battenhouse, '*Measure for Measure* and the Christian Doctrine of Atonement', *Publications of the Modern Language Association of America*, 41 (1946), 1034–5.

3. See Northrop Frye, *The Great Code: The Bible and Literature* (New York: Harcourt Brace Jovanovitch, 1982), 169 ff.

4. N. W. Bawcutt dismisses readings linking Vincentio with God and emphasizes how many of the play's plot elements were found in a 1578 play and 1582 narrative by George Whetstone, both entitled *Promos and Cassandra*, which in turn were derived from Geraldi Cinthio's story collection, *Hecatommithi*. He concludes that 'The Duke remains a collection of attributes which fail to coalesce', because of Shakespeare's technical difficulties in adapting these borrowed plot elements. But Bawcutt's own catalogue of borrowings from secular sources highlights how much biblical material Shakespeare added. Whetstone's only biblical reference is oblique—'Hoc facias alteri, quod tibi vis fieri: you shall be measured with the grace you bestowed on Andrugio'—but it may have served Shakespeare as a prompt. 'General Introduction', *Measure for Measure* (Oxford: Oxford University Press, 1991), 53, 55.

5. G. Wilson Knight, '*Measure for Measure* and the Gospels', *The Wheel of Fire*, 4th edn. (London: Methuen, 1949), 73–96; Battenhouse, '*Measure for Measure* and the Atonement', 1029–59; Sarah Velz, 'Man's Need and God's Plan in *Measure for Measure* and Mark IV', *Shakespeare Survey*, 25 (1972),

37–44; and Darryl Gless, Measure for Measure, *the Law and the Convent* (Princeton, NJ: Princeton University Press, 1979) regard the play as an edifying teaching of Christian doctrine and the portrait of an admirable deity carrying out a biblically modelled plan for human redemption. Clifford Leech, 'The Meaning of *Measure for Measure*', *Shakespeare Survey*, 3 (1950), 66–73; A. P. Rossiter, *Angel with Horns* (New York: Longmans, 1961); and William Empson, *The Structure of Complex Words* (Ann Arbor, Mich.: University of Michigan Press, 1967), 283, see the Duke as a self-serving hypocrite and the outcome of the plot as ironic. Harold Goddard, 'Power in *Measure for Measure*', in *William Shakespeare's 'Measure for Measure'*, ed. Harold Bloom (New York: Chelsea House, 1987), 32, maintains that 'the only way to make the Duke morally acceptable is frankly to take the whole piece as a morality play with the Duke in the role of God, omniscient and unseen, looking down on the world'. Louise Schleiner, 'Providential Improvisation in *Measure for Measure*', *PMLA* 92 (March 1982), 227, counters that the Duke 'is not God but a ruler... whose efforts to imitate God... produce comic results'. A. D. Nuttall, '*Measure for Measure*: Quid Pro Quo?', *Shakespeare Studies*, 4 (1968), 231–51, and James Black, 'The Unfolding of *'Measure for Measure'*', *Shakespeare Survey*, 26 (1973), 119–28, see the play ordered by a comprehensive pattern of substitutions and ransoms based on the Christian doctrine of atonement. Anne Barton, 'Introduction' to *Measure for Measure* in *The Riverside Shakespeare* (Boston: Houghton Mifflin, 1974), 545–9, and Alexander Leggatt, 'Substitution in *Measure for Measure*', *Shakespeare Quarterly* (Fall 1988), 342–59, find that very pattern to be a false lead which falls apart upon close scrutiny, expressing a self-conscious sense of failure by the playwright himself.

6. A number of them are cited in R. G. Hunter's *Shakespeare and the Comedy of Forgiveness* (New York: Columbia University Press, 1965), 211. In fact the biblical penalty applies only to adultery, but later writers often equated fornication with adultery.

7. This gloss occurs at Rom. 9: 15.

8. Northrop Frye, *The Myth of Deliverance* (Toronto: University of Toronto Press, 1983), 37, 30.

9. Some critics claim that this strategy would appear unconscionable to Shakespeare's audience. 'The Duke... is taking on power that's not his own. He gives spiritual counsel... he hears confessions... he is giving false absolutions to people on the point of death', Leggatt, 'Substitution in *Measure for Measure*', 357. But though questionable, such pretence is no more or less transgressive than the false rituals and miracles staged by benevolent clergy in *Romeo and Juliet*, *Much Ado About Nothing*, and *The Winter's Tale*, especially to an audience of Protestants.

10. Louise Schleiner in 'Providential Improvisation in *Measure for Measure*', *PMLA* 92/2 (March 1982), 227.
11. Barton, 'Introduction', 547.
12. Ibid.
13. Schleiner, 'Providential Improvisation', 227.
14. Also, 'Who gave himself a ransom for all men, to be a testimony in due time' (1 Tim. 2: 6).
15. Peggy Munoz Simonds, 'Overlooked Sources of the Bed Trick', *Shakespeare Quarterly* (Winter 1983), 433–4.
16. The gloss states 'he overthrew Satan and the world as with weapons on every side most ready'. Verse 7, immediately preceding 'by honour and dishonour', states, 'by the armour of righteousness on the right hand and on the left'. I read 'on the left' (or 'sinister') as reinforcing 'dishonour' and 'deceivers'.
17. Barton, 'Introduction', 547.
18. 'Heptaplus', trans. Douglas Carmichael in *On the Dignity of Man* (Indianapolis: Library of Liberal Arts, 1965), 69.
19. Wilson Knight, '*Measure for Measure* and the Gospels', 96.
20. Battenhouse, '*Measure for Measure* and the Atonement', 1033.
21. Ibid. 1050.
22. Isabella's final silence may also be attributable to Paul: 'women should keep silence in the churches. For they are not permitted to speak, but should be subordinate, as even the law says' (1 Cor. 14: 34).
23. Leggatt, 'Substitution in *Measure for Measure*', 358.
24. See Josephine Waters Bennett, *Measure for Measure as Royal Entertainment* (New York: Columbia University Press, 1966), and Alvin Kernan, *Shakespeare the King's Playwright* (New Haven: Yale University Press, 1995), 50–71.
25. *The Prince*, trans. Peter Bondanella and Mark Musa (Oxford: Oxford University Press, 1984), 60.
26. C. H. McIlwain, *Political Works of James I* (Cambridge, Mass.: Harvard University Press, 1918), 307.
27. Cited by Jonathan Goldberg, *James I and the Politics of Literature* (Baltimore, Md.: Johns Hopkins Press, 1983), 68.
28. *The Prince*, 55.
29. Ibid. 56.
30. Ibid. 26.
31. Ibid.
32. Post-holocaust initiatives to reconcile present-day Christians and Jews have both acknowledged and obscured biblical divisions that were accentuated in the text that Shakespeare and his contemporaries read. Modern commentators take pains to distinguish 'the Pharisees', whom Jesus

excoriates as hypocrites, blind fools, and murderers (Matt. 23) from 'the Jews' *per se*. But Matthew's description of Jesus's accusers, tormentors, and detractors also includes 'Scribes, Priests and Elders', and he comments that their false discrediting of Christ's rising from the dead 'is noised among the Jews unto this day' (28:15). The Geneva Bible's gloss on this verse reads: 'An extreme vengeance of God, whereby the Jews were the more hardened, so that they cannot feel the profit of his death and resurrection.' For a scholarly argument that Matthew 'felt himself to be a full-fledged member of the Jewish community', see Anthony J. Saldarini, 'Understanding Matthew's Vitriol', *Bible Review*, 13: 2 (April 1997), 32–45. For a discussion of the similarities between Matthew's attack and Jewish prophetic and rabbinic polemic, see Moshe Weinfield, 'The Jewish Roots of Matthew's Vitriol', *Bible Review*, 13:5 (October 1997), 31.

CHAPTER 6

1. Richmond Noble, *Shakespeare's Biblical Knowledge* (London: SPCK, 1935: repr. 1969), 161.
2. Robert Alter, *The Pleasures of Reading in an Ideological Age* (New York: Simon & Schuster, 1989), 116.
3. Ibid. 132–3.
4. See Ch. 5 n. 32.
5. Alter, *Pleasures of Reading*, 134.
6. D. M. Cohen, 'The Jew and Shylock', *Shakespeare Quarterly*, 31 (1980), 53.
7. Ibid. 63.
8. James Shapiro, *Shakespeare and the Jews* (New York: Columbia University Press, 1996), 81–3.
9. 'Biblical Allusion and Allegory in *The Merchant of Venice*', *Shakespeare Quarterly*, 13 (1962), 328.
10. Ibid. 329.
11. This is included in the Geneva Bible's Apocrypha (p. 448) as 'The History of Susanna, which some join to the end of Daniel, and make it the 13 chap.'.
12. Lewalski, 'Biblical Allusion', 342.
13. Ibid. 337.
14. *Shakespeare's Festive Comedy* (Princeton, NJ: Princeton University Press, 1959), 170.
15. 'The Mature Comedies', in John Russell Brown and Bernard Harris (eds.), *Early Shakespeare*, Stratford-upon-Avon Studies, 3 (New York: Capricorn Books, 1966), 224.
16. *Love and Society in Shakespearean Comedy* (Newark, Del.: University of Delaware Press, 1985), 30–52.

17. Lewalski, 'Biblical Allusion', 343.
18. Levin, *Love and Society*, 60.
19. René Girard, 'To Entrap the Wisest', in *Shakespeare's "The Merchant of Venice"*, ed. Harold Bloom (New York: Chelsea House, 1986), 96.
20. Norman Rabkin, *Shakespeare and the Problem of Meaning* (Chicago: University of Chicago Press, 1981), 28–30.
21. Alter, *The Pleasures of Reading*, 131.
22. Richard Elliott Friedman, *Who Wrote the Bible?* (New York: Harper, 1989).
23. See Frank Kermode, 'The Canon', in Robert Alter and Frank Kermode (eds.), *The Literary Guide to the Bible* (Cambridge, Mass.: Harvard University Press, 1987), 600–10, and James Barr, *Holy Scripture: Canon, Authority, Criticism* (Oxford: Clarendon Press, 1983).
24. Robert Alter, *The World of Biblical Literature* (New York: Harper, 1992), 117.
25. Ibid. 129.
26. Michael Gould, 'The Pauline Epistles', in Alter and Kermode (eds.), *The Literary Guide to the Bible*, 489–90.
27. See John Dominic Crossan, *Who Killed Jesus? Exposing the Roots of Anti-Semitism in the Gospel Story of Jesus* (San Francisco: Harper, 1995).
28. *The Book of J* (New York: Grove Weidenfeld, 1990), 14.
29. *Judaism on Trial: Jewish–Christian Disputations in the Middle Ages*, ed. and trans. Hyam Maccoby (London and Toronto: Associated University Presses, 1982), 83 ff., and Jeremy Cohen, *The Friars and the Jews, The Evolution of Medieval Anti-Judaism* (Ithaca, NY: Cornell University Press, 1982).

CHAPTER 7

1. David Stern, *Midrash and Theory: Ancient Jewish Exegesis and Contemporary Literary Studies* (Evanston, Ill.: Northwestern University Press, 1996), 24–5.
2. *Shakespeare: A Life in Drama* (New York: W. W. Norton, 1995), 364.
3. Leonard L. Thompson, *The Book of Revelation: Apocalypse and Empire* (New York: Oxford University Press, 1990), 147.
4. Stephen Orgel, 'Introduction', in *The Tempest*, ed. Stephen Orgel (Oxford: Oxford University Press, 1987), 5.
5. Shakespeare's language here probably derives from a speech by Ovid's witch Medea, but these powers originate with a more primal goddess: 'Hellenistic conceptions of Hekate ... Mistress of the Cosmos ... an obvious rival of the Christ and Christianity ... Hekate and Christ had mutually exclusive franchises on divine revelation ... John ... depicts the risen Jesus as one who has usurped the role of Hekate ... [who was]

explicitly identified with Mene, Artemis, Persephone and Selene... "Beginning and End"... Trivia, she of three roads... who breaks open the earth... the mother of Circe and Medea', David Aune, 'The Apocalypse of John and Graeco-Roman Revelatory Magic', *New Testament Studies*, 33 (1987), 484–7.

6. V. A. Kolve, *The Play Called Corpus Christi* (Stanford, Calif.: Stanford University Press, 1966), 31.

7. John Freccero, *Dante: The Poetics of Conversion* (Cambridge, Mass.: Harvard University Press, 1986), 211–14.

8. Wells, *Shakespeare*, 366.

9. *The Court Masque: A Study in the Relationship between Poetry and the Revels* (New York: Russell & Russell, 1962), 339, 347.

10. Stephen Orgel, *The Illusion of Power: Political Theatre in the English Renaissance* (Berkeley: University of California Press, 1975), 38.

11. Thompson, *The Book of Revelation*, 58; see also David Aune, 'The Influence of Roman Imperial Court Ceremonial on the Apocalypse of John', *Papers of the Chicago Society of Biblical Research*, 28 (1983), 5–26.

12. David Aune, 'The Apocalypse of John and the Problem of Genre', *Semeia*, 36 (1986), 89–91.

13. Cited by Sabine Macormack, *Art and Ceremony in Late Antiquity* (Berkeley: University of California Press, 1981), 18.

14. Gordon Kipling, 'Richard II's "Sumptuous Pageants" and the Idea of the Civic Triumph', in David M. Bergeron, *Pageantry in the Shakespearean Theatre* (Athens, Ga.: University of Georgia Press, 1985), 89.

15. Gail Paster, 'The Idea of London in Masque and Pageant', in Bergeron, *Pageantry*, 53.

16. Stephen Greenblatt, *Marvellous Possessions: The Wonder of the New World* (Chicago: University of Chicago Press, 1991), 16.

17. David Aune, 'The Apocalypse of John and the Problem of Genre', 90.

18. sd means stage direction.

19. Orgel, *The Illusion of Power*, 10–14.

20. Welsford, *The Court Masque*, 340.

21. Stephen Orgel, *The Jonsonian Masque* (Cambridge, Mass: Harvard University Press, 1965), 22–3.

22. This is a variation of earlier biblical stories about tyrants threatening the baby Moses and baby Jesus, both of whom are protected by their mothers and rescued by divine intervention.

23. 'The Song of Moses' (Exod. 15) is the anthem of triumph celebrating the defeat of Pharaoh's armies at the Red Sea (cf. Ch. 4 above).

24. As in Exodus the Pharaoh's firstborn are destroyed as payback for his killing Hebrew firstborn.

25. Like the God of Exodus who hardens Pharaoh's heart in order that more plagues can be inflicted to teach lessons both to Egyptians and Israelites.
26. Paster, 'The Idea of London', 66.
27. Kolve, *The Play Called Corpus Christi*: medieval mystery plays emphasized the grotesque humour associated with Satan. 'Lucifer falls from heaven as a fool who has attempted the impossible and who could have known . . . its fundamental impossibility. . . . Satan makes a fatal mistake in setting under way the plot to kill Christ and hell is harrowed as a result. Anti-Christ is likewise a buffoon, a confidence man' (p. 140).
28. Like the Egyptians who condemn the Pharaoh for continuing to bring down punishments on them.
29. Aune, 'The Apocalypse of John and the Problem of Genre', 84.
30. Orgel, *The Jonsonian Masque*, 39.
31. Like Prospero, in his final speech to Parliament, James abjured some of his autocratic claims in favour of an ethic of reconciliation: 'I will not say I have governed as well as [Elizabeth] did, but I may say we have had as much peace in our time as in hers.' Cited by William McElwee in *The Wisest Fool in Christendom: The Reign of King James I and VI* (New York: Harcourt Brace, 1958), 227.
32. Frank Kermode, *The Sense of an Ending: Studies in the Theory of Fiction* (New York: Oxford University Press, 1967), 88.
33. C. A. Patrides, ' "Image of that Horror": the Apocalypse in *King Lear*', in C. A. Patrides and Joseph Wittreich (eds.), *The Apocalypse in English Renaissance Thought and Literature: Patterns, Antecedents, and Repercussions* (Ithaca, NY: Cornell University Press, 1984), 195.
34. Cynthia Marshall, *Last Things and Last Plays: Shakespearean Eschatology* (Carbondale, Ill.: Southern Illinois University Press, 1991), 114.
35. Orgel, 'Introduction', 56.
36. Title-page, *The First Folio of Shakespeare*, ed. Charlton Hinman (New York: W. W. Norton, 1968), 3.
37. John Heminges and Henry Condell, 'To the Great Variety of Readers', ll. 41–6, in Stanley Wells and Gary Taylor, *The Complete Works*, p. xlv.
38. Ben Jonson, 'To the memory of my beloved, The AUTHOR MASTER WILLIAM SHAKESPEARE, AND what he hath left us', ll. 23–4, 75–6, ibid. xlv–xlvi.
39. James Mabbe, 'To the memory of Master William Shakespeare', ll. 2–7, ibid. xlv.

Suggestions for Further Reading

Facsimiles of Shakespeare's First Folio—*The First Folio of Shakespeare*, ed. Charlton Hinman (New York: W. W. Norton, 1968)—and of the Geneva Bible—*The Geneva Bible, A Facsimile of the 1560 Edition* (Madison, Wis.: University of Wisconsin Press, 1969)—provide evidence of analogous ways these texts were framed, presented, and received during the sixteenth and seventeenth centuries.

Richmond Noble's *Shakespeare's Biblical Knowledge* (London: SPCK, 1935, repr. 1969) contains speculations about which translations Shakespeare read and what his religious attitudes might have been. It mainly consists of a catalogue of biblical references. This catalogue is expanded and updated by Naseeb Shaheen's three volumes: *Biblical References in Shakespeare's Comedies* (Newark, Del.: University of Delaware Press, 1993), *Biblical References in Shakespeare's History Plays* (Newark, Del.: University of Delaware Press, 1989), and *Biblical References in Shakespeare's Tragedies* (Newark, Del.: University of Delaware Press, 1987).

Three short discussions of the topic of this book are found in Roy Battenhouse, 'Shakespeare and the Bible', *The Gordon Review*, 8 (1964), 18–24; Peter Milward, SJ, *Shakespeare's Religious Background* (Bloomington: Indiana University Press, 1973), 85–103; and James Black, '"Edified by the Margent": Shakespeare and the Bible' (Calgary: University of Alberta, 1979).

A number of essays explore significant relationships between individual plays and biblical books. These include Arthur Kinney, 'Shakespeare's *Comedy of Errors* and the Nature of Kinds', *Studies in Philology*, 85/1 (Winter 1988), and Patricia Parker, 'Shakespeare and the Bible: *The Comedy of Errors*', *Recherches semiotiques/Semiotic Inquiry* 13/3 (1993). Russell Fraser explores connections to *As You Like It* in 'Shakespeare's Book of Genesis', *Comparative Drama*, 25/2 (Summer 1991), 121–9. David Evett discusses parallels between the later history plays and the court chronicles in the Books of Samuel and Kings in 'Types of King David in Shakespeare's Lancastrian Tetralogy', *Shakespeare Studies*, 14 (1981). Robert Pack devotes a chapter of his book, *The Long View*, to 'Betrayal and Nothingness: the Book of Job and *King Lear*' (Amherst, Mass.: University of Massachusetts Press, 1991), 251–76. The relationship between *Measure for Measure* and the gospels is studied by G. Wilson Knight in '*Measure for Measure* and the Gospels', *The Wheel of Fire* (London: Methuen, 1949), 73–96 and reprinted in the Signet edition of the play (New York: New American Library, 1964, 1988), 157–85; by Roy Battenhouse in '*Measure for Measure* and the Christian Doctrine of Atonement', *Publications of the Modern Language Association of America* 41 (1946), 1029–59; and by Sarah Velz, in 'Man's Need and God's Plan in *Measure for Measure* and Mark IV', *Shakespeare Survey*, 25 (1972), 37–44. Barbara Lewalski offers a Pauline interpretation of *The Merchant of Venice* in 'Biblical Allusion and Allegory in *The Merchant of Venice*', *Shakespeare Quarterly*, 13 (1962), 327–43. Shakespearian parallels to the book of Revelation are expanded in Chris Hassell Jr., 'Last Words and Last Things: St. John, Apocalypse, and Eschatology in *Richard III*', *Shakespeare Studies*, 18 (1986), 25–40, in C. A. Patrides, '"Image of that Horror": The Apocalypse in *King Lear*', in C. A. Patrides and Joseph Wittreich (eds.), *The Apocalypse in English Renaissance Thought and Literature: Patterns, Antecedents, and Repercussions* (Ithaca, NY: Cornell University Press, 1984), and in Cynthia Marshall, *Last Things and Last Plays: Shakespearean Eschatology* (Carbondale, Ill.: Southern Illinois University Press, 1991).

Helpful literary approaches to the Bible include Robert Alter's *The Art of Biblical Narrative* (New York: Basic Books, 1981); *The Art of Biblical Poetry* (New York: Basic Books, 1985); *The Pleasures of Reading* (New York: Simon & Schuster, 1989); *The World of Biblical Literature* (New York: Basic Books, 1992), and a book he edited with Frank Kermode, *The Literary Guide to the Bible* (Cambridge, Mass.: Harvard University Press, 1987)—a collection of essays by many biblical scholars, one on each book of the Bible. More idiosyncratic but highly stimulating are Northrop Frye's two volumes, *The Great Code: The Bible and Literature* (New York: Harcourt Brace Jovanovich, 1982), and *Words with Power: Being a Second Study of 'The Bible and Literature'* (San Diego: Harcourt Brace Jovanovich, 1990), and Harold Bloom, *The Book of J* (New York : Grove Weidenfeld, 1990). A comprehensive, reliable introduction to biblical study is provided by Stephen L. Harris, *Understanding the Bible*, 4th edn. (Mountain View, Calif.: Mayfield, 1997).

Index

Biblical books are listed as subheadings of 'Bible' in the order in which they appear in the Geneva Bible. Names of Biblical characters are listed as subheadings of the book in which they appear, unless they appear in several books. Play titles are listed as subheadings of 'Shakespeare', with the exception of the five plays treated in detail, which have their own entries. Names of Shakespearian characters are listed as subheadings of the plays.